"I didn't realize how thirsty my soul was for rest until I read this stunning book. Shelly Miller has found a secret door that leads to true rest—a door discovered right in plain sight—and with exquisite prose, she invites you to walk inside. Don't miss this book."

—**Jennifer Dukes Lee**, author of *The Happiness Dare* and *Love Idol*

"Into our culture of chronic tiredness comes a fresh voice in Shelly Miller. This book breaks all your preconceived notions about Sabbath. She makes rest not only obtainable but also the option you'll pick first from a full agenda."

—**Mark Batterson**, *New York Times* bestselling author of *The Circle Maker* and Lead Pastor of National Community Church

"Learning to practice Sabbath has been transformational in my life. It has led me out of striving and simply surviving into deeper grace, joy, and peace. Shelly Miller is extending an invitation straight from the heart of God himself that we all need more than ever in our busy world."

—**Holley Gerth**, *Wall Street Journal* bestselling author of *You're Already Amazing*

"Shelly Miller writes from her soul—one that has been seeking rest in the midst of heavy transition and the busyness of life. She shares with honesty and beauty what she has discovered. What you learn will help you love God more deeply."

—**Margaret Feinberg**, author of *Live Loved* and *Fight Back With Joy*

"For a generation fatigued by the abuse of hurry, Shelly Miller casts a hopeful vision of what life could look like if we learned to receive Sabbath as a gift rather than a rule. *Rhythms of Rest* offers a relieved exhale for the weary, worn-out soul. I'm deeply grateful for this message."

—**Emily P. Freeman**, author of *Simply Tuesday: Small-Moment Living in a Fast-Moving World*

"This book is a labor of love and a gift to all who desire deeper engagement with God's blessing of rest through Sabbath. Weaving personal story with scriptural insight, Shelly writes with a rhythm that gently guides your soul to slow down . . . notice . . . breathe . . . be. Through the years, Shelly has cultivated an online community of faithful friends who practice Sabbath with intentionality. This book brings that community to you and invites you in, with arms wide open."

—**Deidra Riggs**, author of *Every Little Thing*
and *One: Unity in a Divided World*

"Set aside your to-do list. Put off the errands. Ignore the pile of laundry and the dusty mantel. Shelly Miller's *Rhythms of Rest* offers both a delightful respite and life-transforming wisdom you can't afford to miss. Awaken to the gift of Sabbath—God's invitation to rest in him. Let *Rhythms of Rest* be your first step in answering yes."

—**Michelle DeRusha**, author of *Spiritual Misfit*
and *50 Women Every Christian Should Know*

"In *Rhythms of Rest*, Shelly Miller invites us into more than a Sabbath. She invites us into Jesus' heart. She reminds us that rest is really a state of being: of belonging, of knowing we are loved. In a culture wearied by the rat race, Miller's poetic voice is a much-needed breath of life."

—**Emily T. Wierenga**, founder of The Lulu Tree,
a nonprofit based on radical rest, and author
of *Atlas Girl* and *Making It Home*

"Shelly Miller is the rest mentor you didn't even realize you were looking for."

—**Myquillyn Smith**, author of *The Nesting Place*
and co-founder of Hope Writers

"*Rhythms of Rest* is a lyrical, beautiful invitation to experience the peace of heart so many of us desperately crave but can't seem to find. I thought a book on the subject of Sabbath might be a sleeper, but Miller manages to captivate the reader in refreshing and surprising ways. I loved this book!"

—**Heather Kopp**, author of *Sober Mercies: How Love
Caught Up With a Christian Drunk*

RHYTHMS *of* REST

RHYTHMS *of* REST

Finding the Spirit *of* Sabbath
in a Busy World

SHELLY MILLER

BETHANYHOUSE
a division of Baker Publishing Group
Minneapolis, Minnesota

Published by Bethany House Publishers
11400 Hampshire Avenue South
Bloomington, Minnesota 55438
www.bethanyhouse.com

Bethany House Publishers is a division of
Baker Publishing Group, Grand Rapids, Michigan

Printed in the United States of America

Library of Congress Control Number: 2016938466

ISBN 978-0-7642-1843-9

Cover design by Greg Jackson, Thinkpen Design, Inc.

Author is represented by MacGregor Literary, Inc.

16 17 18 19 20 21 22   7 6 5 4 3 2

For H, who embodies a Sabbath heart
and defines rest by the way he lives and loves,
every moment since the day we first met.

A self is not something static, tied up in a pretty parcel and handed to the child finished and complete. A self is always becoming. *Being* does mean "becoming," but we run so fast that it is only when we seem to stop—as sitting on the rock at a brook—that we are aware of our own "isness," of being. But certainly this is not static, for this awareness of being is always a way of moving from the selfish self—the self-image—and toward the real. Who am I, then? Who are you?

Madeline L'Engle, *Circle of Quiet*

Contents

Foreword

Most of us who practice Sabbath came to it slantwise and stumbling. It wasn't some mountaintop epiphany that brought us to the place—it was hopelessness, raggedness, lostness. We were at our wit's end. All our doing had turned into undoing. We had run out of strength and wisdom to manage the wild and yet drab perplexity and complexity of our lives. We had nothing left to give, nowhere else to go.

And then somehow, by some miracle of grace, we heard a voice: *Come to me, all you who are weary and heavy laden, and I will give you rest.*

At the time, we might not have even recognized whose voice it was: we'd grown *that* deaf. All we knew was that our failure to heed the voice would be death. So we came. And we made a beginning, clumsy at first. We weren't accustomed to receiving. We'd lost the art of childlikeness. But slowly, haltingly, we started to breathe again, to feel the hardness of earth and the coolness of water again, to stretch our limbs, to open our eyes, to unclench our fists, to laugh, to cry, to *feel.*

And we discovered whose voice it was: the Lord of Harvest and the Lord of Sabbath. *Eat,* he says. *There is bread to spare. Rest,* he says. *I'll keep watch. Play,* he says. *Stop trying to run the universe.*

Shelly Miller knows all this. Her book bears the sure marks of the desperate. She is not a guru telling us the secrets of enlightenment. She is a fellow traveler telling us where she found bread. Hers is the testimony of the child who lost her way and then, by sheer grace, stumbled unto the only path that leads home and took the hand of the only guide who knows how to walk it. And now she invites us—out of her own overflowing joy and thankfulness—to find that path, to take that hand.

I wrote a book once about my own discovery of Sabbath. Ever since, the practice of rest has become for me a weekly gift of renewal. And ever since, I look for one thing above all in any book on Sabbath: the author's deep—personal, intimate, in the bones—understanding that apart from Jesus we can do nothing. I look for a second thing as well: that Jesus himself, through the author's words, invites us to abide with him.

Shelly delivers on both counts. Here is her testimony of running out of herself and, just in time, falling fresh into the arms of Jesus. And if you attend carefully to that testimony, you will hear Jesus himself calling you. *Are you weary and heavy laden? Are you tired? Come,* he says. *I will show you my ways. I will give you true rest.*

This, I suggest, is why you're holding this book now: to hear that voice, and heed it.

Mark Buchanan
Author of *The Rest of God: Restoring
Your Soul by Restoring Sabbath*

Beginnings

If you keep the Sabbath, you start to see creation not as somewhere to get away from your ordinary life, but a place to frame attentiveness to your life.

Eugene Peterson, *The Pastor*

The week before Christmas, I make a pact with myself: I will sit down and finish writing personal notes in each of several cards lying in a stack on my desk.

These cards were pulled out of a box on the first day of December, along with ornaments for the tree and decorations for the mantel. My aspirations about the holiday season were obviously fueled by idealism. But before I start another project—wrapping gifts, baking cookies, or tidying up the house—I am determined I will finish what is most time sensitive.

Head bent over my desk, I glide black ink over white linen card stock, insert the cards into envelopes, close the flaps, and affix stamps. Momentum toward achieving the goal I created for myself becomes a syncopated rhythm with the discovery of a missing detail: the address for my new friend Susanna. I compose a quick email, press send, and flip the kettle on.

Hi, Susanna,
Hope all is well in your world. I know this is a busy time
for all of us—thinking about you and praying your Advent
has been meaningful. Can you send me your mailing address
when you have a few moments?

I met Susanna during a speaking engagement, a retreat day for clergy wives on the theme of Sabbath. Every time I scoured the audience for responsiveness, I noticed she was sitting on the edge of her seat making eye contact, and either nodding or scribing copious notes in the notebook on her lap. Body language assured me the message I was delivering, at least for her, was indeed relevant. After I returned home, I received a follow-up email from Susanna, a thank-you with an invitation to meet again. I learned that she is not only the wife of a pastor and the mother of two young children but also a published author seeking direction about her next writing project. We have a lot in common. Over the next few months, generous conversations between us echo the spirit of her timely response to my email, words declaring more than I expected.

"Have I been having a meaningful Advent? Amazingly, yes, and it has so much to do with you! Reading your emails has been so life-giving for me." I can almost hear the excitement in Susanna's voice as I read her response and feel my heart begin racing with anticipation.

The emails she is referring to are weekly letters I send to hundreds who make up the Sabbath Society, people who say, "I'm all in" when it comes to making rhythms of rest a reality. The letters are meant to encourage and garner accountability, but often the replies I receive back are more than a thank-you or pat answer to the questions I pose. What I receive instead are accounts of restoration and a surprising return to true self. Susanna subscribed to the Sabbath Society shortly after I extended the invitation to the women attending the retreat day. Susanna's letter to me continued:

I have started taking time each day for that place of meaning and home and rest. I can't explain it, but I feel happier, more at peace, more able to cope, and weirdly, I realized last night right before going on date night with my man, I like myself more. Over dinner, he said to me, "You're energized, it's great, I love being with you."

I feel like I am finding my way, and I don't ever want to go back. Also, I have been having so many ideas; I know creativity thrives in me when I rest. This year has actually been different! I don't know how I can say this, a pastor's wife before Christmas with two kids in school. Also, I have been more organized and actually seem more on top of things. If they could just bottle it and sell it!

She likes herself more? When I initiated the Sabbath Society several years ago, I had no idea I would receive this kind of response to a weekly email. I didn't foresee mentoring people on how to incorporate Sabbath as a rhythm of life. I don't claim special credentials allowing me to be known as an expert on Sabbath-keeping. I'm still learning every day how to rest well myself. What I know is this: In the same way that beginning a New Year with a clean slate and fresh hope motivates us toward change, finding a rhythm of rest in a busy world makes life radically different. Susanna's positive experience is a common outcome among the community, but I pray that transformation never becomes commonplace. Once you open the gift of Sabbath, you will never want to go back to life as usual.

Rhythms of rest are possible because they were there from the beginning. The account of creation in Genesis is our example. When God created the world, he started with a clean slate and fresh vision. Each day incorporated a specific rhythm with rest as the endgame (Genesis 1–2:4).

On the first day, he created light and darkness, and on the second day, he made the heavens. The third day, he created the earth and filled it with vegetation. On the fourth day of the week, God separated day from night, creating signs in the moon, stars, and sun for days, years, and seasons. Can you see the preparation in his mind? The way he organizes time with care toward detail while at the same time anticipating future implications?

On the fifth day, he populated the sea with creatures and the heavens with birds. The sixth day, he made beasts that creep and crawl and walk on the earth, and then he made humankind in his image to have dominion over all the animals. And we think *we* have had a full week!

God stood back and looked at all he had done, rehearsing each previous day of work with the conclusion of deep satisfaction. *Good.* He decided the results of his work had been good. Isn't this how we long to approach the weekend, satisfied with our work and ready for relaxation? Unfortunately, contentment in work that lends permission to rest seems elusive. Our work is never fully finished. And that's why we don't allow time for rest.

According to a study by Oxford Economics, Americans aren't using vacation days and are essentially working for free almost one week per year. Workers are only using 77 percent of their paid time off, the biggest decline in the past four decades. In 2013, the report found that U.S. workers took an average of sixteen days of vacation compared with slightly more than twenty days in 2000.[1] And the reasons why people aren't allowing for time off seem to be common no matter the geography.

Fear of an increased workload once we return, working longer hours in order to keep up with the fast pace, we're worried that other people will assess our time off as being slack, lazy, or incompetent. And even when we do have time off work, we may silence the alarm clock and avoid an office commute, but we often use whitespace to get things done: paint a room of the house, clean the garden until our bones ache, polish the boat, or carpool kids to birthday parties and sporting events. Time off often means we rehearse what we will do next.

On the sixth day, God didn't say, "I'm finished"—full stop—as a justification for a day of rest on the seventh. God is in the business of continually creating, and his work is never fully finished. The work you have to do while you are on this earth is never fully finished either. Sabbath isn't an allowance for rest when the dishes are done, projects are complete, or when your volunteerism is on hiatus.

Genesis tells us that a day of rest was on God's heart long before he made it a commandment. The seventh day is more than a day to sleep in, check out, and be a lump on the couch while binge-watching our favorite TV shows. The day God chose to rest is the first time he names something *holy*.

Holy is unique to God's character, a nature Christians aspire to imitate for achieving moral character. But don't confuse holy with perfectionism in following a set of rules. *Holy* means "set apart," which isn't only limited to people. *Holy* is also used to describe places where God is present. Words like *transcendent, awe, supernatural, fear,* and *reverence* are also used in conjunction with describing the holy.

Holy isn't a word we often use to describe Sabbath in today's culture. We assume a day set apart for rest is impossible, old school, unattainable, not holy. Here is one of many examples I gleaned affirming this notion; a status update from a friend on Facebook.

Well, another Sabbath day arriveth, my friends. The problem I'm finding is that Sundays rarely feel restful and life-giving.

We're hustling and bustling in the morning to get ourselves and the kids ready for church. "For heaven's sake, come here and put your pants on so we can go!" is often said to one or both of the kids every Sunday. And sometimes [my husband] has to say it to me, too.

Then there's church itself, which is always a crapshoot with our kids. It can go fine or REALLY NOT FINE—and usually a crapshoot with me too. Small talk isn't my forte, and every now and then being in church opens up some old wounds that are still healing. So it's a tender time. (I see you, folks who still can't go to church. I see you.)

Then there's lunch after service. We jet home, wrestle [my daughter's] phenomenal stubborn will to get her down for a nap, get [my other child] settled after a high-sensory-input morning, then start cleaning and getting ready to host our small group at 5 p.m. (that can include up to twenty people).

Then there's the kids' bedtime routine. After they're out, I completely crash, only to get up and start the week on Monday, totally drained and wiped out.

SUNDAYS ARE NOT SABBATH FOR ME.

I'm trying to figure out how to honor and practice the art of Sabbath in our home when Sundays look like anything but rest for us.

> *Sincerely,*
> *Drained in Utah*

Sound familiar?

I believe the frustration *Drained in Utah* is communicating is common among many—the assumption that Sabbath is a routine we create. But God created rest to be as natural as breathing. Sabbath is the exhale required after six days of inhaling our work.

Routines are meant to be structured with a specific purpose in mind. Think of dancers, cheerleaders, marching bands, taking the trash out before collection, or even the routine of caring for an elderly person. One small misstep has negative implications and sometimes dire consequences. Routines are often rigid and concrete, correct or incorrect. Usually a person implements rules or follows a routine in order to control a specific outcome. Routines aren't bad; after all, most of us implement a routine of showering, brushing our teeth, and eating three meals a day. We like knowing when the trash will be picked up.

Rhythms, on the other hand, are nuanced and unique to each individual. Rhythms describe the art of living a life embodied with meaning and intention in the same way God creates. The way you move out, adapt to, and integrate with the world around you is like a free-flowing dance of choices. Pay attention to your surroundings, adapt while remaining open to adjustments, and integrate with the world around you. Rhythms shift while remaining focused on what is most important.[2]

A plethora of studies show that the brain requires alternating periods of structured work followed by unstructured rest in order to maximize function. And my friend Susanna is one example among many, proving that in a matter of a few weeks a rhythm of rest is not only possible but life-giving, no matter what your stage of life or circumstance. Sabbath is realistic even when the time you choose to rest is the busiest day of the week. But Sabbath isn't limited to the weekend.

When God made remembering Sabbath the fourth commandment,[3] he asked us to make the day holy and set apart. And when Jesus came to the earth as one of us, he set us free from the law of how Sabbath should look. The commandments are still relevant today because truth never changes; it is always and eternally true. However, Jesus' sacrifice on the cross for our sins changes the rules of Sabbath to a day of grace. He is waiting for us to be with him and to trust that his commandments are good, no matter what day or how much time we choose to give him. Jesus *is* Sabbath. When we make the day different on his behalf, holiness inhabits our intentions.

A few years ago, during Advent, I stumbled upon Sabbath only to find *awe, transcendence,* and *reverence* aren't just words describing the God we know from Genesis, but a common way of experiencing him when rest is the focus. The unexpected surprise we open each week is like a letter sliding into your inbox: personal, generous, and more than you expected. Rest isn't only a choice we make from a menu of options, but rather the focus of our time set apart from work.

Whether a rhythm of silent pauses at your desk, a couple of hours to quiet thoughts midweek, or a whole day to play and ponder on the weekend—when we choose a rhythm of Sabbath, everything changes. You may even like yourself more.

But first, you must choose to begin.

CHAPTER ONE

Baby Steps

The Sabbath is not for the sake of the weekdays; the weekdays are for the sake of Sabbath. It is not an interlude but the climax of living.

Abraham Joshua Heschel, *The Sabbath*

I don't do guilt. As I stare at the time beaming from the screen of my phone, those words push to the forefront in the cacophony crowding my thoughts.

In a pleather chair, my husband sits next to me, and on the other side, a row of strangers. Scrolling through emails and social media, I intermittently look up, hypervigilant as people walk through security pulling suitcases. It's the third week of Advent, and my mother-in-law, Geri, left Phoenix and is flying on windwings heading east. She'll land at dusk at Myrtle Beach. I prepared for her arrival with clean sheets and twinkle lights decorating the headboard in the spare bedroom; wrapped packages with gift tags bearing her name lie underneath a decorated Christmas tree. Celebrating the season begins when she pulls her carry-on through the living room. In all the preparations for her presence with us, I didn't have time to buy groceries. Now after her long, tiring day of cross-country travel, we have to stop for food on the forty-five minute drive back home.

I don't do guilt. It's the mantra I adopted from my mother-in-law more than twenty-five years ago when I became one of her children, a phrase as familiar as her welcoming blue eyes and the accepting smile we witness as she walks through the gate. I come from a long line of Catholic guilt in my ancestry. A spiritual mutt, I was discipled by the Baptists, infused with the spirit of the Pentecostals, embraced by the nondenominational melting pots of mega churches in the Midwest, and now, serving as an Anglican and the wife of a priest, I find that I still need to practice her words often.

We share many fond memories from Geri's extended stays with us, whether resting at our family cottage in Canada for summer vacation or celebrating holiday seasons. But storytelling around the dinner table is one of my favorite activities when she visits. With one ear tuned to Grandma's stories and the other to the commotion around us, our teenagers, Murielle and Harrison, sink into their chairs to quietly listen. We are equally riveted as if it's our first time hearing about Miller family antics.

No matter how many times Geri retells stories of traveling and adventure, my kids never seem to tire of hearing about their dad as a teenager, fresh with new driver's license in his back pocket on the Autobahn, speeding like a professional race car driver. But on this visit, we hear a new story over plates of spaghetti, one of our last meals together at a restaurant before she flies back home to the desert.

She tells us about an evening out with a family at a private Jewish dinner club. As they choose seats around a table, the hostess escorts her young son to the bathroom. Geri notices a lighter next to the candles on the table, and before she sits down, she picks it up, flicks it on, and sets each wick aflame. When her friend returns to the table, horror is written on her face.

In Jewish tradition, on Sabbath, the eldest woman of the house recites a blessing over the candles no later than eighteen minutes before sundown: *I am the light of the world. Whoever follows me will never walk in darkness, but will have the light of life.* After lighting each candle, the woman moves her hands in a circular motion three times as if bringing the warmth of the flame closer in and then recites a blessing: *Blessed are you, Lord our God, King of the universe, who sanctified us with his commandments and commanded us to be a light to the nations, and who gave us Jesus our Messiah, the Light of the world.*[1] Geri had no idea how many minutes were left before sundown that evening and she assumed they would pray over the meal once each person took a seat around the table. A thoughtful gesture she assumed was helpful turned into an embarrassing situation she will never forget. Over bites of pasta, laughter erupted in unison as we listened to her honest, self-deprecating portrayal regarding the mishap.

Guilt is one of the main roadblocks for making Sabbath a reality. Guilt about the things we leave undone, and guilt when we don't rest perfectly. Lofty expectations about a day set apart for rest keep us immobilized, and Sabbath elusive. Guilt is usually a sign that you've made rest a routine with strict rules. If you struggle with guilt about taking time to rest, then perhaps you are trying to implement a Sabbath routine instead of a rhythm of rest.

When we adopt Geri's mantra, *I don't do guilt,* a simple act can become sacred when we ascribe meaning to it, separating the mundane from the holy—reciting a special prayer, lighting a candle, and preparing different food from the usual fare. Sabbath, I learn, is a sacred day separating what is most needful from the smorgasbord of options on your plate. We will feel as though we don't exactly know how to do it right, but the mystery will woo us back to light the candles the following week. Through practice, we discover the discipline of rest doesn't require a special anointing or particular stage of life.

On Saturday, after Geri flies back to Phoenix, I begin cleaning up evidence of celebrating for two weeks and make room for

Christmas dishes to be stacked back in the china cabinet, moving plates and fragile keepsakes behind doors underneath. I push a silver coffee urn gently beside a row of champagne flutes and grasp delicate Shabbat candlesticks, one in each hand. *Shabbat* is a Hebrew word used for Sabbath, which means "to cease." We must cease in order to rest.

Slowly sliding one of the fragile candlesticks on the dining room table, I am careful not to take any chances of breaking them. Placing the other silver bottom upright in the palm of my hand, I hold it above my head toward sunlight streaming through the high dining room window. The hollow blue glass in the middle becomes translucent, light revealing imperfections. Turning it around slowly, I admire the bubbles and streaks of pigment unnoticeable behind glass. I inspect the decorative silver flowers wrapped around the candle cups like a lab technician looking through a microscope. The creative artistry piques curiosity about the meaning behind the beautiful craft.

"Hey, why aren't you using the candlesticks I bought you?" H asks as he saunters through the living room, back to his recliner. (Yes, my husband's name is only one letter; more about that later.)

He caught me. The truth is, when H came back from a trip to Israel and gently unwrapped each gift he'd picked out for us, it seemed as if he'd read my mind when I saw the candlesticks he bought for me. That same year, I read *Mudhouse Sabbath* by Lauren Winner. Her perspective on the ways Jewish tradition enhances a Christian pilgrimage renewed expectancy I had allowed to go dormant. I hadn't nourished what God had planted in my heart. Handling those candlesticks germinated what had been forgotten like a green shoot poking through the hard earth after winter's frost had passed. My soul remembered what my mind forgot. But God waited until the petals of those initial thoughts about Sabbath were fully open after Christmas to capture the full aroma of something important he was planning to birth. His timing is perfect, even when it sometimes feels as though he has forgotten or is busy with something more important.

With every day closer to the end of Christmas vacation, I find myself exhaling repeatedly, pushing air through what feels like a straw in my chest. On this last Saturday before resuming our workaday life, simple tasks become weighty. I push the vacuum cleaner under the table, sucking up glitter and pine needles while imagining swimming in the lake at our family cottage in Canada, hearing the call of loons through the open window and watching fog roll over canoes upturned on the beach.

● ● ●

My mind goes back to the previous summer. A towel is wrapped around my waist over a damp swimsuit, my go-to outfit at the cottage. As we gather at the faded yellow island in the kitchen for lunch, I slice summer sausage and cheese and serve it on blue Melmac plates next to a pile of crackers. Murielle and Harrison curb their immediate hunger with plump green grapes from a bowl.

Earlier, bare-chested boys in swim shorts meandered through the woods between the family cottages—sandy-haired cousins in search of Harrison for a ride on the four-wheeler. We were all congregated next door, welcoming family members visiting from Germany, entertained by the bilingual accent of youngsters swinging in the hammock. Listening to tales of backpacking through Europe from one, and the missionary journeys to the Amazon from another, our newest addition to the family, Noah—married in from Uganda—kept us engrossed with stories of competing in the world swimming championships alongside Michael Phelps after teaching himself how to swim as an adult.

"I'll come over after lunch," Harrison yells to the boys through the screen door. They quickly scurry off, bare feet padding through the tall grass strewn with dandelions.

Leaning into the back of her chair at the table, Murielle tilts her head slightly and remarks, "We have an international family, don't we? I never realized that for some reason."

H and I look at each other, responding with smiles and nodding. Tales of adventure and risk for the kingdom inspire us toward the fulfillment of hope. Cultural diversity awakens something dormant in both of us. We long to experience the vastness of the world's people through traveling, yet feel left behind in the tiny seaside village where we live. It's a curiosity we've kicked around for nearly ten years—why God moves us to places where the intimacy we long for in community remains absent.

"Hey, how would you define belonging and fitting in?" H asks the kids on a whim from the kitchen sink. One bare foot inside the dining room and the other on the porch, Harrison pushes the screen door open, chewing the last of a cookie. "Belonging is being accepted for who you are, and fitting in is changing who you are to be accepted."

I am dumbfounded. My teenage boy, growing into manhood, nails it.

Brené Brown describes it this way: "Fitting in is about assessing a situation and becoming who you need to be in order to be accepted. Belonging, on the other hand, doesn't require us to change who we are; it requires us to be who we are."[2]

Busyness bullies with a false message of fitting in, something my adolescent son already knows at a young age. Most of us have believed the fallacy the world advertises: achieve, produce, and earn success in order to gain acceptance, love, and ultimate happiness. But the more we fill our lives with yeses, even noble and good ones, who we are slowly drifts into obscurity until all that remains is a shadow of our former self, void of purpose and definition. When we believe there is never enough time to do everything, we become aimless and forget why we are here on the earth. "Everything is wearisome beyond description. No matter how much we see, we are never satisfied. No matter how much we hear, we are not content," writes the teacher in Ecclesiastes (1:8 NLT). Sabbath reminds us that we belong because we are already accepted. Rest requires that we be who we are and nothing else. A life built upon Sabbath is contented because in rhythms of rest we discover our time is full of the holiness of God.

For two weeks at the cottage, we wake up late and sit in our pajamas under the spell of Round Lake and the distant call of loons. Change into swimsuits when the sun takes her high and lofty place. Shower only when necessary, and walk to the store dripping wet and indulge in high-calorie snacks before dinner. Forget what day it is until asked, and only use mirrors for small glimpses of imperfection when the mood strikes. Self-doubt stays on the bedside table with our cell phones without service. We are only aware of time when the sun begins her descent and the breeze tickles the skin, signaling twilight and cocktails. Star-gazing for constellations, satellites, and shooting stars remains a mainstay on the bucket list in Canada, no matter how sleepy we are when someone notices the twinkling curtain overhead on a clear night of darkness. We watch, schooled by the mystery.

Surrounded by family members who accept immature mistakes and forgive the proclivities of childhood, we learn to relish our differences. And find new confidence in our identity.

I used to think a two-week vacation away from the crowds on the Internet was a necessary respite, a return to our hidden state. I thought our true selves emerged when cast away from life's busyness, but now I know differently. Our time at the cottage is a magnification of what true belonging looks like when we choose rest as a rhythm of life.

Even in the grasp of community, we can feel like misfits, with brief stints of warm belonging blowing through the open windows of our lives. But home is not a structure; it is a place that resides within each of us. We long for that place to be bigger than our experiences and without expectations about popularity or acceptance by the masses. We find that place of belonging while resting in what I have come to learn was God's intention from the beginning.

As I finish vacuuming under the dining room table, the sun descends, coloring every room in the house amber. Golden fingers creep through shutter slats and woo me to come out. I leave Christmas ornaments strewn in collections throughout the house, plastic bins from the attic open and waiting. *One final walk around the neighborhood to soak up the Light will help me breathe,* I think. Every step becomes a prayer tug-of-war, a conversation of questions and answers between us.

Jesus, you have brought me to a place where belonging is absent. Because I believe you don't make mistakes, how can I feel peace in belonging, the same way I do at the lake—or the inner contentment I feel at Christmas, surrounded by family? How can I experience inner rest and a lack of loneliness that lasts for more than two weeks?

Sabbath. It's the word I hear rumble through my bantering. Pulling the zipper on my sweatshirt up to my neck, I walk up a hill a bit slower in contemplation.

Sabbath? Of course, why hadn't I thought of that?

Before Christmas, I had purchased *Wonderstruck,* written by my friend Margaret Feinberg. I savored a chapter every Sunday during my quiet time, but it was the fourth chapter, "A Sanctuary in Time: The Wonder of Rest," that haunted me most.

Margaret writes,

> *With rest, I noticed God-moments I might have missed before. My prayers grew clearer. Studying the Scripture became more meaningful. When life was rushed, I felt like I was reading a cookbook backward—nothing connected or made sense. Now I felt more attuned to God's voice in the Bible.*
>
> *Sometimes you have to slow to a stop and reset before you can experience divine presence. My hunger to know God increased as I learned to develop a healthy rhythm in life and rediscovered the wonder of rest.[3]*

She is describing how I feel when I'm on vacation at the cottage and on holiday surrounded by family, but can I really experience this every week? Remembering and keeping the Sabbath is a commandment, but perhaps I've viewed it as an elective, something to choose if and when the opportunity suits my schedule. Some associate Sabbath as a day of guilt, a time for stifling fun, but this hasn't been my perspective while growing up. Honestly, it seems as if Sabbath might be a setup for disappointment like a New Year's Eve resolution of diet and exercise in order to achieve maximum health. Good intentions fueled by a hopeful clean slate will result in feeling like a failure if I cheat or stop prematurely. I need help and accountability.

Invite people to join you. The next thought pushes through the debate I am having with myself as I walk around our neighborhood. A man smoking a cigar passes me. We nod to each other, smile, and offer the typical polite southern wave. Cords from my earphones lay over my chest, but the music is turned off.

Yes! I can invite people to join me through my blog. Any discipline is easier to achieve with the encouragement and accountability of community. We can try this together as an experiment and see what happens.

When I return to a warm house, my cheeks are rosy—not because they are cold from my brisk walk but because God met me intimately, answering my longings, doubts, and questions with new perspective and holy anticipation.

"How was your walk?" H asks without moving his head away from a football game blaring through the television.

I tell him about newfound hope, my curiosity about Sabbath, and what I sense may be a new direction I am to take. He looks at me, nods in agreement, affirming I should do it.

As darkness descends and stars begin to twinkle, I place the Shabbat candlesticks on the granite island in the kitchen, a prominent place in the open floor plan of our house. Candles in the cups, I light each wick and watch the golden flames flicker in tandem with my heart pulsating peace. Unfinished projects remain on the dining room table, dirty dishes in the sink; the vacuum cleaner remains parked next to the bare Christmas tree. I sit down in the recliner, push it back, and prop up my feet. Closing my eyes, I exhale and welcome rest like a visitor unpacking a suitcase. Rest is staying for more than two weeks.

A few hours later, lounging in the same place in front of the television, surrounded by my family, sans a computer on my lap, I turn to H and chuckle.

"This is so hard for me," I admit a bit sheepishly.

To-do lists scroll through my mind. A conveyor belt holding thank-you notes without addresses, an incomplete editorial calendar, emails awaiting responses, and blank lines on a grocery list, not to mention the plastic containers of Christmas tchotchkes.

"I know," H affirms, "but this is good. It's the first time you've been engaged with the family like this in a while."

His honest admonition is a sobering reality check and confirmation resolving my inner conflict. A few hours of rest is not just for me but an allowance for overdue, uninterrupted presence with my family. *I don't do guilt.* I can hear Geri saying it to me even though she is back in Phoenix.

Busyness can be avoidance instead of preparation. We've been busy with lots of things—running errands, decorating rooms, cleaning up messes, and cooking special food, all in preparation for receiving guests, celebrating Christmas, and making moments festive. Every*thing* might be ready, but emotionally, psychologically, and spiritually, *we* are not. Ironically, busyness in the wrong things ultimately leaves us completely unprepared for what is most important. Choosing to leave practical things undone is a brave act of trust and relinquishment. And relinquishment often precedes the miracle. Advent is our example.

Advent is a season pregnant with hope and expectancy, weeks of preparation for contemplating and then receiving the miracle of Jesus' birth. Advent welcomes the incarnation into every home of those who celebrate it, but along with it there is the tension about the choices we must make. Will busyness define how we wait for Jesus to come? Or will quiet contemplation be our sweet surrender while we wait? Similarly, Sabbath asks not "What will you give up for him?" but "How will you wait for him to come?"

Advent prepares us for the birth of Jesus, but also instills mindfulness about the second coming. And Sabbath, like the season of Advent, allows us to wait with expectancy. Waiting can imply mindlessness, boredom, wasting time, passivity—even hopelessness. But in Hebrew to *wait* also means "to hope."[4] As we wait, God reveals his purpose in the preparation he is doing within us, and our hopeful outlook is the result. Sabbath invites Christ to come into our everyday life, to rethink priorities and celebrate his faithfulness. Sabbath is weekly preparation and anticipation for making space in our lives for Christ to come. Sabbath rhythms are generous gifts: they are not about guilt.

Busyness can also be a sign that trust is faltering and the fear of scarcity is taking over. Fear that there won't be enough time to get everything done if we take a day off to rest. Exodus reminds us that when we obey the commandment of Sabbath rest and trust God with our time, he is faithful to provide what we need:

> On the sixth day, they gathered twice as much as usual—four quarts for each person instead of two. Then all the leaders of the community came and asked Moses for an explanation. He told them, "This is what the Lord commanded: Tomorrow will be a day of complete rest, a holy Sabbath day set apart for the Lord. So bake or boil as much as you want today, and set aside what is left for tomorrow. So they put some aside until morning, just as Moses had commanded. And in the morning the leftover food was wholesome and good, without maggots or odor.
>
> 16:22–24 NLT

You know what happened when some of them tried to save a little manna just in case God didn't come through on other days? The next morning the manna was full of maggots, smelling putrid.

On Saturday, I run last-minute errands, prepare a meal that will provide leftovers for Sunday dinner, and tidy up the house. When the sun goes down, whatever I haven't finished stays undone for twenty-four hours. If I am tempted to fold one more load of clothes, clean the bathroom sink, apply another coat of paint to that piece of furniture, or answer those last few emails, I become like the Israelites, compromising by making excuses that stink. A lack of faith in Sabbath reeks of self-sufficiency. And the fear of scarcity robs us of the miracle.

Moses warned the Israelites,

> Eat this food today, for today is a Sabbath day dedicated to the Lord. There will be no food on the ground today. You may gather the food for six days, but the seventh day is the Sabbath. There will be no food on the ground that day.
>
> Exodus 16:25–26 NLT

But they still didn't believe him. They went out searching anyway, and guess what? There was no manna. All that time looking, scavenging, searching for something to satiate their hunger, but they came back empty. "I observed everything going on under the sun, and really, it is all meaningless—like chasing the wind" (Ecclesiastes 1:14 NLT).

You must rely on yourself—this is the lie of scarcity that bullies us into thinking Sabbath is not realistic.

"[You] must realize that the Sabbath is the Lord's gift to you" (Exodus 16:29 NLT). He gave the Israelites a double portion so they would know that he is enough, and he will do the same for you.

For most of my life, Sunday ended up being a weaker version of the rest of the week. I took a nap or read a book after attending church, but I usually pulled back to "producing" after I had those few hours of rest—cleaning up whatever was left undone from the week. But Sabbath isn't about resting in order to be more productive. It isn't about me at all. One day a week, God asks us to "Remember the Sabbath day by keeping it holy" (Exodus 20:8) because he knows how easily perspective can slant. That's what I tell my blog readers in the first week of January, and forty-two people sign up to practice Sabbath with me. Those who are skeptical but curious write to me first.

"So what's the Sabbath Society entail? Give me the scoop!" My friend Michelle sends me an email from Nebraska with this simple question.

"OK, here's the skinny," I write back. "I decided to observe a true Sabbath and then began thinking about how any discipline is a bit easier when you have encouragement along the way. I know finding time to rest is hard and that's why so many of us pass over it. I thought I would invite my readers to join me this year. I'll send out an encouraging, honest email with some resource links about Sabbath every Friday morning. I will throw out a welcome mat and you'll have a choice about replying to me personally, or not. The welcome mat is there regardless. No pressure, no jumping through hoops, no guilt. Just encouragement and affirmation that you don't have to be alone in it if you don't want to be."

"This sounds awesome, Shelly! Sign me up—I need the encouragement!"

January 11, 2013

Hello Everyone,

I really wanted to do a personal email to each one of you because that is normally how I roll. But this is about Sabbath and keeping things simple as we make our way toward rest. So this is an inaugural email to welcome you to the Sabbath Society. I'm so glad you said, "I'm all in," and decided to join me.

A few of you have asked questions about time commitment and what you need to do to be part of the group. My answer is: That is completely up to you.

My plan is to email you every Friday with some encouragement, some ideas that will make you think differently about Sabbath—at least that is my prayer. I'll ask some questions about what works for you, what doesn't work, and where you are struggling . . . you get the picture. You are welcome to read the email without replying or reply to me personally (the icing on my cake). My hope is that we will encourage each other by our own successes and failures as we navigate Sabbath together.

This isn't about perfection or achieving sainthood. It's about linking arms, knowing that what we gain in the observance results in transformation as we focus on Peace. And that is the goal of this pilgrimage of faith, right?

And let me tell you, we'll have to fight for this time. Right now, I'm sitting down while dinner bakes in the oven. I'm hoping to tie the bow on two writing projects before sundown tomorrow. Life is full for all of us.

This is how I'm preparing for a successful Sabbath this week: I went grocery shopping last night for easy meals from sundown on Saturday to sundown on Sunday. This may not sound like a big deal, but I rarely grocery shop at night. I know some of you may choose another day; it doesn't matter.

I'm making a Crock-Pot meal on Saturday for dinner that will (hopefully) provide leftovers on Sunday. Unless they gobble it all up, in which case we'll order pizza.

I'm pre-scheduling my weekend blog post and turning off all social networking sites beginning at sundown tomorrow. This is harder than just flipping a switch or clicking on tabs to close them, let me tell you.

And I'm not doing anything that involves creating more work for me. No emails, no taking notes for a Bible study while I read, no writing blog posts, no grocery lists or organizing closets. So when I have a nudge to do something productive, I'm asking myself, "Is this necessary?" This takes some major restraint, and my husband is keeping me focused.

I'm not trying to create legalism. This is a discipline for me that will hopefully become a habit. What about you?

How will you approach Sabbath? There is no right or wrong answer here.

Until next week . . .

> *Walking with you,*
> *Shelly*

Responses pour in confirming we all struggle with the same issues when it comes to rest, but my friend Sherri sobers me the most when she writes back. For those who struggle with a lack of margin in life, Sabbath requires surrender and deeper trust.

With so much of my time consumed by work outside the home (full-time 9 to 5:30, then part-time from 6 to 10), Sunday and Monday are the only time I have to do housework, laundry, and catch up on regular responsibilities. Rest is a much needed luxury that I'm sad to say I haven't gotten much of lately. I've been doing housework on Sunday, and then I have somewhat of a rest day on Monday. However, since I began practicing "restful" Sabbaths, I've sort of swapped my days. My baby steps are taking a little time each evening to do a load of laundry so it isn't such a pile at the end of the week. Also, I've started to shop for groceries with recipes in mind that can be prepared ahead, or frozen even, then popped in the oven . . . baby steps.

Starting is the hardest part of any good intention toward creating new rhythms. We begin a little uncertain, doubting we'll be able to rest because of the work stacking up. But the more we plan the path and organize the journey, the more we will begin to walk our days *toward* Sabbath instead of away from it. And just like the Israelites, as we practice taking our hands off creation, we begin to believe God is trustworthy while we put faith into action.

The basis for making our days meaningful and filled with purpose comes with considering this question first: What and who are your priorities? If Jesus is top on the list, then this is a helpful exercise for making rhythms of rest a reality. Take a long look at your calendar from Wednesday to Wednesday with Sunday as the centerpiece, or the day you choose to Sabbath if Sunday doesn't work for you. Whatever day you choose to Sabbath, walk each of the four days beforehand toward a day of rest as the focal point so that preparing for Sabbath becomes the high priority among myriads of options. Instead of compartmentalizing rest, Sabbath becomes integrated as a lifestyle along with the people and circumstances that are most important. And if a whole day seems impossible, begin with a window of time that works for you.

Maybe Sunday is your day to rest but it often begins hectic, rushed, and results in a day that isn't peaceful. On Saturday, lay out children's clothes, put a meal in the Crock-Pot, tidy up the house, leave dishes in the sink at sundown, and use paper plates when you wake up. Baby steps.

Perhaps Sunday obligations make rest difficult. Find a window of time on another day of the week. Take a long prayer walk alone or with the dog, linger long in pajamas while savoring a cup of tea and journal random thoughts. Baby steps.

You work two jobs and fall asleep when you finally sit down? Take your lunch hour in a peaceful spot alone, once or a few times a week. Listen, write down what you hear, and practice adoration.

You may not have time for a whole day to rest, but a small window of time here and there cultivates a Sabbath heart. Pausing for prayerful listening, even for a few minutes, brings everything that is important back into focus. We need whitespace for hearing the truth more clearly.

Beginning is always the hardest part. Whatever time you choose to Sabbath, wipe the minutes clean of work. No answering emails, starting new projects, or ordering groceries online; no reorganizing drawers or polishing shoes. What brings you joy and peace and closer to the heart of God? Your answer will help to define what rest looks like for you. Rhythms, unlike routines, bring intention toward our choices and order back from chaos. A life of intention ultimately leads to deep satisfaction.

A few weeks later, Michelle writes, "I love these emails, Shelly—thank you for taking the time to do this! As I was just doing my crunches (ow!), I thought, *I can't wait for Shelly's Sabbath email today!* and when I opened my in-box, it was there."

Like Michelle, finding a rhythm of rest for me began with a bit of curiosity leading to further investigation about the truth. God began wooing me toward the epiphany of Sabbath as I embarked on that providential walk. Eight months later, on another summer vacation at the cottage, I arrived in Canada curious about the future and our livelihood. Once again, one simple word changed everything. Except this time, the word wasn't as straightforward as *Sabbath*.

CHAPTER TWO

Questions and One-Word Answers

Does one never sleep except to let something else awake?

C. S. Lewis, in a letter to his friend Mr. Greeves

I awaken to the squawking staccato of geese congregating on the shoreline, a slight breeze blowing through the open window. Eyelids slowly open to sunlight illuminating curtains from the back. My fingertips brush over the empty place on the mattress, a topography of wrinkled cotton sheets worn from years of use, still warm with H's body heat. A curious word echoes through the entrails of my dreamscape: *writ*. Words are my passion, but I've barely uttered this one in four decades. *Writ*. It's the only word I remember as I awaken.

Throwing the covers down to my ankles, exposure to the brisk morning air prickles the skin on my arms and legs. A welcome reminder of our timely escape from the stifling humidity we left looming over the driveway two days ago. I turn my mind toward scooping up meaning from the remainder of words floating in the soup of my first morning thoughts, but instead of clarity, more questions surface, making the contents murky.

Why *writ?*

I've learned with repetition that those first few moments before fully awaking from a sound sleep aren't always the result of the spicy food I ate or an unresolved conflict my brain is attempting to solve while I sleep, but rather divine hints for a new path and fresh direction toward destiny. I'm paying attention.

On the first day of a two-week respite, my excuses for distractions are limited. The pen and journal I packed in my bag now lay on the nightstand, ready for inspiration's impulsiveness. I scratch my thoughts out quickly, but what I heard plainly while dreaming becomes lost the more I awaken.

Writ. The word haunts me.

Nine in the morning? No, it couldn't be! Already? I pick up my reading glasses lying next to the clock, double-checking with clearer focus, when I'm startled by a slight jostling of the doorknob. A thud from the bottom jolts the door open, swinging it wide before it ricochets off the edge of the plaid couch. H stands in the doorframe, holding a steamy mug of fragrant coffee, catching the bounce of the door with his elbow. He's the third generation in his father's side of the family to embrace the curious one-letter name that incites lots of questions. We decided to stop with a fourth. Harrison, my son, has an H name but without the legacy of the family history attached. Paradoxically, my daughter Murielle is named after her maternal grandfather, Murrell, and her paternal grandmother, Muriel. Later, we discovered that what we thought was an inventive namesake is actually common in France.

Dressed in red ball cap and sweatshirt with *Canada* in white letters over his chest, H has already made coffee next door in the cottage while the house sleeps. The glint in his eyes reveals the boy once called Sandy by his grandmother. He's returned to the place associated with long summer days of youthful abandon.

"I can't believe I slept in this late," I tell him, leaning against a pillow headboard in the garage suite with books on my lap. "Are the kids awake?"

"No, they're still asleep; we have two teenagers, remember? It's beautiful out there," he reports, "not a cloud in the sky and the lake is like glass."

Two days ago, we left our seaside town in South Carolina, trading the suffocating humidity and typical everyday worries stuck to our agendas to push pavement twelve hundred miles north. As native Pat Conroy writes, "South Carolina is a state of contained, unshared intimacies. It is a state of crosscurrents, passwords, secret handshakes, but it rewards the lifelong curiosity of both natives and strangers alike."[1]

This vacation is the knot on the end of the necklace strewn with busyness and work. The secure spot of family tradition I roll my fingers around most every summer since H and I said, "I do." H's family cottage is the clasp holding six decades of Healey family history, and a reminder to all of us that we belong even when our accomplishments threaten to become our identity.

Pushing bare feet through the legs of my yoga pants, I choose a walk with my camera instead of flipping buttermilk pancakes. I pad through the damp grass toward H, who returned to a lawn chair in the gazebo after waking me up, long legs propped up on a picnic bench, open Bible in his lap. Chipmunks dart across the lawn, startled by my intrusion, and scurry up thick layers of pine bark. Their scratching ascent breaks open a canopy of stillness. H turns toward me. We lock eyes, communicating without saying anything.

The hems of my soggy pants brush my ankles, sending chills up my spine. Grass confetti sticks like static electricity to my shoes with each step. I stop and stare at the horizon; my hand covers my squinting eyes, an awning shielding the brightness. I've memorized this moment for eleven months, breathless with the reality.

Captivated by simple beauty, I sit down and mentally retrace the familiar lines of the landscape.

Water gently laps on the shoreline, the sun illuminating the lake surface like a flash mob of photographers. Children's voices and the hum of a boat echo from miles across; the blue cloudless sky meets inky, indigo water. A bird trills from two houses beyond, breaking my trance, diverting my attention toward the beach strewn with sand toys, water skis, and crumpled beach towels. I hear myself exhale. And think, *In this familiar place, the clock is no longer a bully but a favor. With years of practice, I've learned that vacation is a change in mindset cultivated by the inspiration of new geography. The choice of rest is a kindness to your inner self that is desperate for conversation about calling.*

Though our time at the cottage feels like an escape from work, we carry the friendship of Jesus along with us, knowing he desires our wholeness more than a quick fix for unrest. He wants us to discover how he is afoot in the everyday moments of life, not only the days we allot for vacation. Quiet conversations and contemplation during times of rest bring the core of what matters most in life bubbling back up to the surface.

A few years ago, seated on this same beach, I read the words of Madeleine L'Engle from *Walking on Water*. Words that still linger with definition:

> Kairos. Real time. God time. That time which breaks through chronos with a shock of joy, that time we do not recognize while we are experiencing it, but only afterwards, because kairos has nothing to do with chronological time. In kairos, we are completely unselfconscious, and yet paradoxically far more real than we can ever be when we are constantly checking our watches for chronological time.[2]

Her book is now a staple in my tote bag every summer.

L'Engle's words remind me that I am here not to check out from reality, but to do business with my Maker. He is asking questions that are not rhetorical, bringing me to a safe place of familiarity for wrestling through answers.

"What do you want me to do for you?" It's a question Jesus asks his disciples James and John, and the same one he asks of Bartimaeus, a blind man sitting on the side of the road.[3] It's straightforward; it's simple, isn't it? It's obvious how a blind man would answer that question, but Jesus wants to hear him say it with specificity and without reservation. He's asking you and me the same question when it comes to making rest a rhythm. How will you answer?

His question brings opportunity for digging deeper, answering with vulnerability, wrestling between truth and fiction and choosing trust over self-protection. And like a father asking his children, God wants us to tell him what we want. Instead, we slump our shoulders in ambivalence. Mark Batterson writes, "If faith is being sure of what we hope for, then being unsure of what we hope for is the antithesis of faith, isn't it? Well-developed faith results in well-defined prayers, and well-defined prayers result in a well-lived life."[4]

I want the legacy of a well-lived life, don't you? I'm learning to say what I want with greater clarity and definition, even when it feels uncomfortable and presumptuous, because I don't want a mediocre life as a result of vague prayers and ill-defined faith. When you are tired, depleted, worn out, and weary, imagine Jesus asking, "What do you want me to do for you?"

When we are tired, coming up with an answer to that question seems monumental, doesn't it? Even rest is a vague answer: an answer that leads to vague results. In a culture of busyness, most of us live in the tension of unresolved solutions for continual cycles of chronic tiredness. We know we need rest, but struggle with finding margins.

The question "What do you want me to do for you?" is at the heart of making rhythms of rest a true reality. In the same way, you and I are intentional about what we are going to eat for dinner, graphic when teaching our children how to dress, detailed about decorating our homes, and defined about our roles in the family. When it comes to rest, Jesus wants you and me to tell him what we want with specificity. Truth is not trite; it has texture and tenacity to it.

We embrace intentions for work, academics, relationships, finances, recreation, and faith, but what about intentions for rest? Most of us don't spend time thinking about how a day of rest might look in a busy week. We don't dare to dream about rest outside of paid vacation time because a whole day for resting seems unrealistic, so far out of reach that pondering the possibilities feels futile. As a result, we block out the possibility of rest altogether. Intentions about rest seem silly, unnatural, an extravagance in wastefulness, especially with to-do lists strung out over every room in the house. Rest is ill-defined when we value time and our worth based on productivity.

If we are created with intention by God for a specific purpose, and the way of discovering that purpose is through relationship with him, then the way of discovering what we are missing in life is through abiding with him on Sabbath. A lack of intentionality when it comes to how we rest leads to a depleted life defined by what the world dictates. When we are overtired and dreading the alarm clock, we miss out on the hints toward happiness God is leaving for us. "Wasting time" is actually the most productive action you may take this week.

What would wasting time look like for you right now? Curling up with a page turner? Instead of flipping through the latest issue of *Vogue*, perhaps lingering over each page? Chatting with a friend on the phone for more than a few minutes? Meandering through a park without looking at your watch? Perusing a new haunt your friends are Instagramming?

"Do not oppress a foreigner; you yourselves know how it feels to be foreigners, because you were foreigners in Egypt" (Exodus 23:9). While "wasting time" is foreign to the DNA of a culture that often values what we do over who we are, Jesus understands more than anyone the uncomfortable place Sabbath creates within us. He understands because he once stood in our shoes. Choosing Sabbath requires faith and trust, but the outcomes experienced aren't only for you.

One of the ways God instructed the Israelites in how to live was by setting up a weekly Sabbath. And then, for the good of man and all he created, God patterned a sabbatical year after that Sabbath rhythm. "For six years sow your fields, and for six years prune your vineyards and gather their crops. But in the seventh year the land is to have a year of sabbath rest, a sabbath to the Lord" (Leviticus 25:3–4). In the same way Sabbath reminds us who it is that controls all the details of life, God reminded Israel that he is the true landowner, and all they possess ultimately comes from him. Every seven years, land was to lie fallow, and what grew up without work was reserved for the poor, those who wouldn't have enough resources for food.

"Six days do your work, but on the seventh day do not work, so that your ox and your donkey may rest, and so that the slave born in your household and the foreigner living among you may be refreshed" (Exodus 23:12). When we trust God by taking our hands off our work, what we give up through Sabbath ultimately benefits those around us.

As my friend Susanna makes changes in her personal life to make Sabbath a reality for her family, the people who work alongside her and her husband are reaping the benefits as well. Every seven weeks, instead of gathering for routine staff meetings at the church, they meet somewhere else—a park, restaurant, movie theater—and spend a fun day together:

> *Honestly, it's the best decision we've ever made in terms of leading our staff. Our only objective is to cultivate relationship, but the irony of taking a day off to rest is that ultimately we become better equipped to serve people.*

Jesus waits for our undivided attention like a tender father, a gallant gentleman, a friend who is interested not in what we can do for him but in how he can love us. He gave his life, the price for our freedom (Mark 10:45), yet often we choose to define value and worth by what we produce and shackle ourselves with a bulging agenda. Living by faith is a continual conundrum. There is dissonance between the reality of life challenges and the definition Jesus gives for real living. But faith isn't a static, one-time commitment or a magic intellectual decision erasing life's problems. Faith is a brave surrender, an unwavering commitment to trust in a Savior who takes care of the details despite hurdles and hardships. He longs for us to trust him with rest as much as the other parts of life.

Will you trust him by "wasting" time? What would that look like for you right now? Saying no to a volunteer request? Leaving dirty dishes in the sink? Waiting a few hours or a day (gasp!) to answer emails collecting in your inbox? Are you willing to risk the discomfort of responsibilities piling up in your absence while you connect with your Maker?

Walking down the familiar dirt road behind our cottage, I think about the things I left undone in order to rest with my family on vacation. Past a nylon tent and a clothesline waving with dry swimsuits, I inhale the trails of a smoky fire, the smell of bacon popping in a camping skillet. Conversations echo through a cavern of morning stillness in the park adjacent to our family property. As I meander toward the Bonnechere River, a small boy stands alone on a floating weathered dock, casting the line of his fishing pole into clear water. The plop of the hook signals a human presence among nature. Birds chatter perched on pine branches. I stand beside an overturned red canoe propped against a large tree trunk, frozen while looking through the lens of my camera in wonder and thankfulness.

Lord, thank you for this beautiful place. Thank you for providing a way for my family to be here every summer. For the legacy of sacrifice by Grandfather and Grandmother Healey, who made this respite a reality for generations to gather. I trust you with all the knowns and unknowns surrounding my life, knowing you control outcomes, working all things together for our good. You are generous, loving, and faithful.

Like the boy repeatedly casting his line into deep waters, I recite rote prayers from my childhood, look through my lens in search of wonder again, and wait for a nibble—a small glimpse of hope that God has something for me, even though I can't always see it.

When the mind is focused entirely a problem, we lose sight of God's place within it. We pit ourselves against all the details as if the problem is ours to conquer immediately. Anxious and tense, we can wrongly assume that unless we achieve total victory, we will lose the battle and defeat will be our legacy.

Sabbath provides space between you and your problems, enabling you to see from God's perspective, often with surprising results, like a word breaking through your questions about life and awakening you to something more important. God is always near, but we often dismiss his powerful presence in the midst of pain and hardship.

There is a tendency to interpret God's voice in the midst of uncontrollable circumstances with an antidote that worked last week—a cure someone with similar symptoms discovered with success or a Bible verse to fit preferred outcomes. And in our search for greater insight and deeper meaning, the busyness of acquiring solutions keeps us from entering into the sacred space where life springs forth. When we stop searching, the power of deceit diminishes. Sabbath is an awakening—a space of time containing reminders about what is most valuable. We will have trouble in this world, but Sabbath reminds us we will always have Jesus. All he asks is that we quiet our inner voices insisting on results and trust in the riches waiting for us in rest.

Framing life's circumstances through the lens of Sabbath is a reorientation, a quieting of inner dialogue with an outcome of broad perspective, different from a routine quiet time or leisure activity. Waiting for Jesus to come, to define purpose in the midst of circumstances that don't make sense, ultimately determines the path we take. Relinquishment of a preferred outcome precedes the miracle of fulfillment.

A frog croaks from beneath an overturned canoe, strumming through the quiet like an out-of-tune guitar with a broken string. It makes me chuckle. The melody speaks to me in a way only God knows my heart will notice. I've spent much time concerning myself with what people think, making calculated decisions about my career based on the fickle propensities of the market, choosing prudence over risk. That frog isn't concerned about how I perceive his gift of music; why should I be? God created the frog to croak and hop. He is relishing in his identity. And this is the simple outcome of Sabbath: God's nearness becomes palpable, singing all around us. Elevator music suddenly becomes a symphony of distinguishable notes the more we make rest a rhythm in a busy week. We realize that who we are, right here in this moment, matters to God because we are created in his image. We glorify him best when we accept who we are without reservation.

What are you missing because you are too busy to notice?

Stop. Right where you are. Close your eyes and listen. Can you hear the whir of the refrigerator, a siren in the distance, a bird chirping from a branch outside your window? I'll wait. Go ahead.

Now open your eyes and look up. What do you see? Billowy clouds floating across a blue sky, or cracks in the ceiling? If hurry and hustle have long defined your stance, it is possible that you have missed the awareness of God's presence amidst your circumstances. Your inability to decipher what he is saying has caused his voice to become muffled, or worse, a deafening silence. But when we rest, even for a few moments, we can hear his voice with greater clarity.

I want to shout my belonging as a friend of Jesus like the frog croaking poetic. I want to wear who I am like a garment. *Stop expecting others to dictate the words of your story*, I hear him echo. *Pay attention to the chapters of the story I'm giving you.*

In the breezeway, we stand in a circle dressed in new Roots (Canadian brand) sweatshirts, holding hands with sleepy family members who rise early to see us off. Handing over keys to the front door, I swallow the lump in my throat and hug each cousin, aunt, and uncle with well-wishes. The symbiotic sacredness of the circle somehow welcomes hopefulness. Bowing together, we pray for safe travels and a return next year with the same fervor.

Tires *da-dum, da-dum, da-dum* over cracked asphalt, road signs for each state blurring past as we move swiftly south. New York, Pennsylvania, Maryland, Washington, DC, Virginia, and onward to our South Carolina address, exhausting my peace and sense of belonging with each mile.

Surrounded by suitcases, water skis, and golf clubs in the back seat of the van, worship songs bellow through the speakers. The words and melodies hearken back to three months earlier, when H and I first heard them. We were worshiping among thousands in the Royal Albert Hall in London, attending the Alpha Leadership Conference. During those days, we surrendered work to listen to leaders and quiet our thoughts. And God reawakened a long-ago call to England through what we were hearing spoken from the platform and in the songs of worship.

I envision the petite woman on stage singing the song now coming through the van speakers, strumming a guitar strapped across her shoulder and resting on her hip. *Spirit of God, fire of love, come have your way in us . . .* and tears threaten to fall. Reliving the moment of providence H and I sensed about our future, I envision a bustling community of faith in London alive with creative inspiration and flourishing with culture, a place where our hearts ache for the broken and those who search for meaning and purpose in the wrong places.

Is the desire a vain imagination? Or hope pushing us forward? These are questions I've asked repeatedly as I ponder and wait. And perhaps my prayers have been vague and unspecific in this area too.

Looking out the opposite window, I watch trees swoosh past, and a semitruck pulls alongside, making my mouth drop open. *ENGLAND,* bold red letters painted on the side of the truck, keeping pace with our car for more than a few seconds. We're traveling through the southern region of the United States; what are the chances? Overcome with emotion, I keep the coincidence to myself and continue looking out the window.

Is this my answer? It seems silly that God would choose to answer my daydreaming questions through a logo on a truck. But why wouldn't he? He can do anything he wants. Coincidence? It seems almost laughable that I would see the word *England* the same moment I'm thinking about being in London.

Why not? He seems to be using words to garner my attention. But I wouldn't have noticed the serendipity had my heart been busy and distracted.

As I begin writing down what happened in a journal on my lap, I notice a missed call on my cell phone. It's a message from my best friend, LuAnn, who lives in Kansas:

> *I haven't read anything online that you've posted recently, but I feel God is giving me a word of hope for you from Ephesians 2:10 in the Amplified Bible: "For we are God's handiwork, recreated in Christ Jesus, that we may do those good works which God predestined for us, that we should walk in them." I wanted to share this because you keep coming back to my mind, in case it was something you needed to know as you make your way back home from Canada. I sense you are going home to Christ, not South Carolina. He is who and what you are traveling back to, and I sense he wants to encourage you with a message of hope.*

I leave summer's winsome affection in the rearview mirror and move into the season of fall with anticipation. *Writ.* That curious word suddenly comes back to the forefront of my thoughts like a rubber band let go after being pulled taut. I won't feel the sting of intended definition until months later, at home, in front of my computer.

Chapter Three

Prayers and Epistles

God is a novelist. He uses all sorts of literary devices: alliteration, assonance, rhyme, synecdoche, onomatopoeia. But of all these, His favorite is foreshadowing.

Lauren Winner, *Girl Meets God*

"All his precepts are trustworthy." On the weekend, I read Psalm 111:7 at my writing desk before the others stir from sleep. That short phrase tucked away like a jewel among life's litter captures my attention. I keep scrolling back to the revelation. The word *trust* found me with the turn of the calendar, declaring a triumphant theme for the year. It feels hopeful somehow, not daunting. And everywhere I wander *trust* echoes as if shouted in the Grand Canyon. The word bounces back to me. *Trust me in your writing, in parenting your teenagers, in the unknown journey with your husband into the future*—that is the message trust carries with it in my heart.

And perhaps the more something dangles like a carrot in the forefront of your thinking the more you can't help but be hungry for it in the morning quiet of a Sabbath. I take a gulp of lukewarm tea from my cup and set it back on the coaster without moving my eyes from what I'm seeing.

He reveals his intention of *writ* (that sleepy morning at the cottage) through the portal of the word *precept* in the dictionary. Now I'm stuck on the word in the verse from Psalm 111. I'm not sure I fully understand the meaning, so I look it up, more alert than on that first day of vacation.

A precept is "a general rule intended to regulate behavior or thought . . . a writ or a warrant," I read from Oxford.[1] And there it is again, that curious word I didn't understand out of context. Now God has my full attention. I continue on a word scavenger hunt: "A writ is a formal written document; specifically: a legal instrument in epistolary form issued under seal in the name of a sovereign."[2] The Ten Commandments are the writs God instructed Moses to chisel into stone for our good. In Hebrew, the Commandments are called *aseret hadevarim*,[3] the ten words or the ten utterances; words that guide our intentions, thoughts, and actions.

If his precepts are trustworthy, then his rules are for our good, not imprisonment. Right? But what is the meaning of that word *epistolary*? I haven't seen it lately in a sentence, and words pique my curiosity like a feline drawn to catnip.

"*Epistolary* is relating to or denoting the writing of letters or literary works in the form of letters, from the Greek word *epistole,* meaning 'a letter'"[4] (*epistle* being the English form). And that's when the revelation grabs me and shakes me from sitting cross-legged and dumbfounded.

He has dropped the *e* on *write* and let it dangle for weeks. I am a writer who is commanded to lead an expedition, a mission to help others listen for his voice while resting through weekly epistles to the Sabbath Society.

This is much of life, isn't it? An unintentional meander that stumbles upon meaning for our curious questions through a circuitous route—a promise defined by linking serendipitous events together. Or, wait a minute. Perhaps the serendipity is providential, like hints guiding a forager to find sacred truth among trash. "It's your heart, not the dictionary, that gives meaning to your words" (Matthew 12:35 MSG).

If God is cataloging our stories in the Book of Life (Revelation 21:27), and his precepts are trustworthy, then our conversations with him are the epistolary, an intimate story of friendship told by an omniscient narrator, the ultimate romantic. His words for us aren't just for discipline and pointing fingers. They are personal love letters with his fingerprints on the edges, words written in unmistakable voice. Language making the heart race wildly with purpose.

Maybe that's it! I've mistakenly equated the fourth commandment with his index finger wagging in front of my face. Instead, his stance on Sabbath is arms wide open and waiting for me to run into his embrace. Sabbath is a personal epistle from Jesus with news about your life.

An epistle from Jesus isn't for safekeeping or only for reading during hardship, loss, doubt, or conviction, but rather an intimate nearness, a whisper tucked away in your heart. An unspoken dialogue at unexpected moments, doing mundane tasks, when we believe his precepts for us are trustworthy and he cares about what we care about.

Conversations with our Creator encompass meaning and purpose, the lifeblood that brings our stories to birth. Interchange with our Creator—it's a choice, an elective he hopes you'll pick first from the list that is keeping you busy. "He waits to be wanted," writes A.W. Tozer.[5] And because God is a gentleman—not pushy, showy, or fickle with his presence—he courts desire from beneath the layers we create for protection. Not to manipulate emotions but to cradle purpose with strength and power, when you are ready for surrender to the weight of it.

It is a revelation, says John the Revelator, that Jesus stands at the door and knocks, waits for the invitation to enter because he honors relationship (Revelation 3:20): a relationship that causes your flesh to faint and other aspirations to wane once you give yourself over to it.

Sabbath is an invitation for intimate conversation. It is an intentional quieting, transforming information into tangible experience, into words and sentences that harness our purpose and calling.

"It is no surprise," writes Frederick Buechner, "that the Bible uses hearing, not seeing, as the predominant image for the way human beings know God. They can't walk around and take God in like a cathedral or an artichoke. They can only listen to time for the sound of God—to the good times and bad times of their own lives for the words God is addressing to, of all people, them."[6]

The word *writ* seems random, a lexical wallflower forgotten beneath mounds of overused vocabulary, like stagnant prayers and repetitive conversations with the One who is fluid and knows what we are thinking before we form our thoughts.

When we envision our relationship with Jesus as a never ending love story fueled with anticipation, it changes the way we approach tomorrow, the future, and the way we walk toward Sabbath. During the week, I often talk to H with my back to him if my hands are in soapy dishwater. I don't have to look him in the eyes when we talk about the events of the day because I know he is listening as he affirms and interjects throughout our meandering conversations. I once heard someone say that the longer you're married to your spouse the less you make direct eye contact. When you know someone intimately, you don't have to look them in the eyes during every conversation. Still, there are times when eye contact is required. You know, those random moments when you overspend at T.J. Maxx and compromise the bank account, when someone voices an opinion that is different from yours, or when you're out on a dinner date huddled over a flickering candle. Those times in a relationship require attention and single-minded focus, showing love by listening attentively. Sabbath is a weekly dinner date with Jesus, a time set apart when we give him our undivided attention.

May I propose that our lives are a series of love letters to our Creator? A continual conversation that started the day we took our first breath. Sabbath is a special time he anticipates because he loves you. We prepare to be with people we love by choosing the right outfit, making reservations, considering preferences, and anticipating conversation. And we prepare for Sabbath in the same way. In order to rest in the presence of God, we think ahead and consider the ways we can make the time both meaningful and memorable.

For some, it may mean planning activities that keep the kids occupied, playing quietly while you rest. Planning beforehand what you will need for the day so you aren't running errands during the time set aside for rest.

Sometimes my conversations with H aren't about our relationship but the needs of others we love and influence. When we share details about someone's pain and suffering or the joy they are experiencing, we give each other the opportunity to speak into the situation from our unique viewpoint based on experience and wisdom. It is the same when we pray for others. Jesus often responds to our personal prayers directly, and sometimes we incarnate love letters from his sacred mailbox for others, delivering timely messages to those who are waiting for answers.

Rest provides fine-tuning for hearing God's messages amidst the static of life. Passing on the messages he sends for others without distorting the meaning can sometimes prove to be risky. Sabbath-keeping provides good practice in discernment. I learned that with Jody.

"Since you are asking for prayer requests, can you pray for my daughter Leah," writes Jody. "She's in her seventh year of marriage and newly pregnant. My daughter is experiencing some complications—a subchorionic hematoma between the baby and her uterus." Jody explained the scenario for her daughter: regular visits to the midwife and emergency room, bed rest, ultrasounds, and finally quitting work to protect the health of her baby.

Jody noted that her daughter's complications were curiously colliding with the timing of her own recent job loss. Now available to help with chores and doctor visits, she became an empathetic presence for her daughter when it would have been previously impossible.

"Will you pray for things to even out—that the placenta will reduce to normal size and the baby will grow?" she asked.

Leah is Jody's only daughter. She describes her as practical, levelheaded, ordinarily transparent with her feelings. But a mother's intuition was telling her that the stress was beginning to wear her daughter down.

Jody and I exchange emails a few times a month, though I've never met her in person. Our relationship started in the comment box on my blog, then later on social networking threads. Our email conversations began with prayer requests as a response to my weekly Sabbath letter, when I asked how I could pray for people.

During the twenty-four hours away from routine tasks—housework, errands, writing, and emails—I carve out some time for listening prayer, focusing on those who respond to the letters with requests. I'm often expectant because God's presence seems different, multiplied in closeness somehow, much like what the Jews refer to as a second soul that comes for a special visit on Sabbath.

As I close my eyes, it's as if I've entered a movie in progress. Beautiful images of places I've never seen before scroll through my mind, intermittently freezing a random frame into a portrait I linger over. Phrases and words bubble up through the images, offering clarity to my prayers and admonitions. Often I am a third-party messenger, carrying the surprise of redemption in an epistle God asks me to pass on to someone else.

As the sun begins to rise on my Sabbath, rays of light streak across the wall of my office. Sitting at my writing desk, I click through emails while praying for each struggle, disappointment, and hardship, writing back when something stirs my spirit, burning for release.

That morning, I received nothing in particular for Jody. No impressions, just peace and silence, the sound of birds chirping outside my window. It was later, seated at Sunday service, that a clear message came to me.

During worship, my mind wandered down a tree-covered path seen through the window. Inventing stories about adventure, I suddenly begin paying attention to where my thoughts are taking me—a discovery that the jaunt isn't a careless meandering but the way to a secret garden where a message is hidden. Ignoring the crescendo of lyrics rising to the rafters, I write down the metaphor God is giving me. I don't want to forget the message for Jody:

Sometimes there are things in the way of giving birth, not just practical things but spiritual. They are there, swelling beneath the surface and we are unaware of them. But they keep us from growing into the fullness of God's plan for our life. I sense God saying you will be a midwife to spiritual birth for your daughter, freeing her from what might be hindering her growth. I also sense that your job loss and this circumstance with your daughter is not a coincidence. God has linked the two events, the two of you, for his purposes.

I caution Jody to pray with discernment to see if the metaphor resonates with her circumstance. I take the words God gives me seriously, but I'm human.

I am heartened when Jody tells me her daughter is drawing closer to Jesus. Linking hearts over the next few weeks at a distance, I pray with Jody through more complications with Leah's pregnancy. After a grueling three-hour doctor's visit, the adversity brings the confession of a breakthrough for Leah and her husband as they sob over the phone explaining to Jody how they have begun surrendering the growth of their unborn child to Jesus. Their heart response to difficulty is evidence of God's compassion to those on the sidelines. Jody writes,

By no coincidence at all, the photo on the January page of their new calendar is a drawing of a mother's very large

tummy with the faint outline of a baby inside and a large hand coming down from heaven, touching the mom's tummy, and the words "I knew you before you were born."

I posted a picture on Facebook about a week ago of the plaque on the counter in her midwife's office with the exact same words on it . . . and I took that picture before Christmas.

God is clearly speaking through it all.

She is capturing the serendipity, the sacred echoes God is sending through her anxiety and stress. God's face seems to be shining on Jody when, a few days later, she sends me this note:

Shelly, my precious Leah lost her baby boy on Friday night, and we've been planning the memorial, texting, emailing, and making phone calls to family and friends. It has been a sad but gloriously miraculous time, watching God unfold in her life, just as you shared Jesus would do.

Afterward, I heard Jody's voice for the first time when I answered my cell phone while writing at my desk. Buried in a mound of details for the memorial service while grieving the loss of her unborn grandbaby, she was awestruck by how God's redemption interlaced throughout the sad circumstance. In the final moments of our conversation, Jody mentioned a follow-up appointment with the doctor for Leah resulting in a discovery. Her uterus is shaped like a heart.

"Perhaps God is saying there needed to be a spiritual birth before wrapping their arms around a baby," I remarked in a moment of discernment, "and you were the midwife to the arrival."

Silence lingered between us.

"I never thought about that," she said, her voice shaking through her sniffles.

Sometimes your life is a glorious waking up to the perfect temperature; a gentle breeze blows through the open window in your bedroom, and sips of coffee are savored. Morning headlines proclaim hope for a change and traffic moves at a swift pace.

But on other days, your awakening is from being so hot the sheets stick to your skin. Everything you think about threatens to suffocate your hope. Each swallow of coffee hurts because of the lump in your throat. Instead of finding inspiration in your surroundings, you must work hard, like panning for gold in order to find what is most valuable.

On many days, my life resembles the latter. The predictable nature of our surroundings creates an inner boredom and discontent that produces a question I ask God often. How long? How long must we wait in this place while the tug of my heart remains relentless toward England?

The discontent isn't a surprise to God. For a big chunk of our marriage, H and I have been curiously entangled with the culture and love of all things British. We have several long-term friendships in England, and the dream of being not just occasional visitors but residents is at the top of our bucket list.

About twelve years ago, after tucking our young children into bed, we sat on the couch in our living room, making plans for celebrating an upcoming wedding anniversary. Prices plummeted on airfare to Europe, allowing us the dreamy option of an overseas celebration among other possibilities. We longed to visit our British friends with whom we shared years of spiritual growth in community while serving together on staff with Youth With a Mission (YWAM). After lengthy debate, weighing the pros and cons of such a decision, we prayed together. Peace didn't come alongside our reasoning. In fact, what happened was similar to what I experienced with Jody.

As I closed my eyes to invite Jesus into our decision, in my mind's eye a moving truck appeared with an open bed, possessions crudely tied with rope to wooden slats. I was the passenger in a car following the truck through the streets of London, passing familiar landmarks, when suddenly we came to an American stop sign immediately before an underpass. Everything I was seeing halted like pausing the frame of a movie. Breaking through what I was seeing, there was an overriding mental image: *Not now, but later.*

Despite longings and low airfare, those words and the vision translated a clear message about not going to London for our anniversary. But the vision and the words still hang over the mantel in my memory. We've made many trips to London since, and each time we walk the city streets our hearts become a tempestuous sea of unrest. We long to live among the people, not just visit. With each new place we tour in England, God churns the waters of desire and passion. Instead of fighting the feeling, we choose to surrender and trust him for the fulfillment of what was planted all those years ago. Trust that as each piece of our story unfurls, we will understand his purpose and intention with the clarity of history.

With each passing week, I practice Sabbath, and peace replaces unrest. The words of Isaiah become my comfort, "Only in returning to me and resting in me will you be saved. In quietness and confidence is your strength" (Isaiah 30:15 NLT). Along with restoration, I experience what the Jews refer to as the *neshamah yeteirah*, an extra soul that comes to dwell with us on Sabbath but departs once the week begins. In Hebrew, the verb *havdalah* means "to separate," and Jews use the term in reference to the separation of Shabbat from the other days of the week. There is, in equal parts, expectancy and sadness in havdalah.[7] The extra soul the Jews describe is an out-of-the-ordinary intimacy in relationship I experience that is different on Sabbath than the other days of the week. A nearness that allows me to hear with abnormal acuity and obtain an unusual peace. The presence of God is not a matter of distance, but experience.[8] And when that sweet experience ends at sundown on Sunday, sadness comes along with nightfall. But the grief, I come to realize, is what draws me back for more Sabbath. Like a lover I am smitten, heartsick while waiting for the return of sundown next Saturday.

The Lord says, "I will guide you along the best pathway for your life. I will advise you and watch over you" (Psalm 32:8 NLT). Noticing what bubbles to the surface of our thoughts in times of rest can be a saving grace, the beginning of a love letter Jesus is sending. And sometimes, not only for you but for someone who desperately needs rescue, hope, or assurance. Don't wait until the last epistle in this chapter is sent before capturing what you hear your soul saying in times of stillness. Chronic busyness results in soul amnesia, the thief stealing life-giving moments of *neshamah yeteirah*, the extra soul that dwells with us on Sabbath.

Listen to your life, and then respond to what you are hearing. Collect the epistles God is sending like a scribe poised with an open notebook, jotting down sacred echoes. Transcription may not seem logical at first, but stay attentive, open, and faithful. As I learned through my experience with Jody, a daydream may not be so random after all, but a mental jaunt down a pathway opening up hidden truths for someone. Another encounter as a result of listening prayer came through Sandi in California. She responded to the letter I wrote to the Sabbath Society offering to pray over requests.

Dear Shelly,

I so enjoy your letters. They remind me to carve out time for Sabbath. My greatest joy in the past few weeks has been seeing the seeds of faith that have been planted over the years grow and even bloom in my college-age son. He has encountered a few health issues that caused him to need to leave a dream behind. He has verbalized that he doesn't know what God is doing but that he trusts God to have a plan that will benefit him and bring glory to God. What more could a parent want? Joy beyond words.

Sandi from Orange County

Dear Sandi,

So glad to hear from you. We love Orange County. I just wanted to tell you that I felt led to pray for your son this morning and was overwhelmed with a wave of emotion. I felt the Lord say that your son should know that the path for his life is not re-routed, a do-over, or an alternative because of health issues. He is and always has been with him through every step. I saw a dotted line being colored in and asked the Lord to begin to connect the dots, revealing to your son the places where he didn't recognize God at work in and around his life, places where he assumed God was absent but was actually orchestrating and loving him all along.

Just wanted to share what I was sensing in prayer. Perhaps it resonates.

Lots of love to you,
Shelly

"Wow, I read your email on Sunday morning and cried," admits Sandi. "The thought of someone else loving my child by bringing him before the throne of Jesus was overwhelming to me. It also caused me to wonder if that is how God feels as we pray for one of his children. Does he just well up with love and gratefulness?

"I printed your email for my son. The timing was perfect. God's timing always is perfect. Thanks for not just taking the time to pray, but for also sharing it with me. It was encouraging beyond words."

Sandi followed up with me six months later telling me her son landed well, is a happy college student, healed of a health issue, and very aware of the presence of God in his life. Sharing those mental notes with others requires some risk and bravery, but God's reputation and the outcomes are his business. All he asks is that we trust him and remain faithful.

Three portions of Scripture reveal three ways we can respond when sensing the Holy Spirit is saying something to us that requires action.

In the book of Acts, Priscilla and Aquila listen to Apollos preach the gospel from limited knowledge about baptism. Afterward, they lovingly take him aside to explain the truth more clearly and broaden perspective. Sharing wise counsel fueled by intimate knowledge of Jesus, the couple mentors Apollos, not because they are know-it-alls setting him straight but because they care about the way the truth is communicated.[9] They love those who are hearing the message as much as the message itself.

When it comes to discerning the ways God speaks to us, a wise heart accepts correction and seeks counsel from those who are further along in faith.

In the gospel of Mark, Jesus spits on a man's eyes as a method of healing his blindness. When the man describes seeing people walking around like trees, Jesus touches him a second time with the result of clear vision.[10]

Sometimes what we hear during listening prayer isn't a clear answer the first time we ask for direction. Clarity isn't always instantaneous, but comes as a result of persistence, perseverance, and practiced faith.

Further in that chapter of Mark, we learn how Jesus communicates plainly to the disciples the fact of his coming death and resurrection, leaving no room for misinterpretation. Yet the disciples don't want to hear the truth Jesus is telling them.[11]

There are times when what we hear from God for ourselves and others isn't what we expect or hope to hear. Times when the answers we receive translate into disappointment or hardship that is painful, yet we must accept what he is saying.

Our days are a collection of moments that make life beautiful. In our busyness, we tend to see life as one giant bouquet given by the Creator and miss the details in each flower he's picked out for us. Sabbath helps me take account of where Jesus has been afoot in my days and notice the details with heightened awareness.

A few months later, as the leaves begin turning golden, another letter from Sandi comes into my inbox. Upon reading the first line,

I gasp and place a hand over my heart. "I wanted to recount to you how I believe Sabbath saved my husband's life."

Sandi is a full-time children's director at her church, meaning Sunday is a workday for her. Inspired by ideas on preparing for Sabbath from several Sabbath Society letters, she began making soup on Saturday, putting bread in the oven on Sunday, and using the remainder of the day as a time to allow God to pamper her heart. But when she received an email from an old friend whose husband had committed suicide two years earlier, she decided to use that time to visit her friend instead. She sounded weary. But when Sunday afternoon came—bread warm out of the oven, soup hot on the stove—she cozied up in a special place and decided to postpone the visit with her friend. And that decision to stay put and rest well turned out to be providential.

While Sandi was abiding deeply—reading, praying, and listening to the delightful sound of family throughout the house—she was startled when her husband called out to her. He was yellow, sweating, and telling her he did not feel well. A trip to the emergency room resulted in the discovery that Sandi's husband was in the midst of a heart attack. A blood clot had traveled to an artery, causing 100 percent blockage. Choosing rest meant Sandi was able to get her husband to the hospital, a timely decision that saved his life:

> I impress upon my children not to just get through the tough times but to learn from them. There is learning and work to do in each season of life, and if we learn well and work hard, we go into the next season more prepared and aware of God's presence and purpose. For my husband and me, this past year has been a very long and bleak winter season. We see little fruit; it often feels dark and cold; I have needed and been nourished through Sabbath-keeping. Times of quiet and stillness before the Lord have allowed me to see pieces in the puzzle that make up our lives. In full assurance that God is always in control and that this heart attack was another piece

in the puzzle gave me peace that surpasses understanding. The winter fog and cold has not lifted. Our future is unknown, but I have great anticipation and excitement about the ways he is going to work all this out. He has prepared me to be here and he is here with me.

Sabbath is a reminder that there are no last chances with Jesus. In Christ, each day is a new beginning of "hello" and "I love you." And all of his precepts are trustworthy.

CHAPTER FOUR

Dispelling Myths

In such places, on the best of these Sabbath days, I experience a
lovely freedom from expectations—other people's and also my
own. I go free from the tasks and intentions of my workdays,
and so my mind becomes hospitable to unintended thoughts:
to what I am very willing to call inspiration.

Wendell Berry, *This Day*

"I always knew there was something different about you," Galina
says in a thick Russian accent. She is dressed in her usual black,
the uniform of women who work behind makeup counters in retail
stores. After open-heart surgery, her white hair is cut very short.
Her blue eyes twinkle behind black-framed glasses as we catch up
on her health issues.

Her surprising comment comes after inspecting the business
card I hand her, at her request. "You have a presence about you
that I couldn't quite put my finger on, but now I know what it is."

Galina is one of several familiar faces working in the cosmetic
section of a favorite department store in a city near our small

seaside village. Whenever these beautiful women spot me among crowds of shoppers, they call out my name, greet me with a knowing smile, and wrap their arms around me. Satiating a growing curiosity through my recurring visits to their workplace, they ask about recent trips I've taken to London, inquire about the kids, and then finally ask what they can do to help me with product selection. H has learned that this is his time to peruse the men's department or another store entirely in the mall.

While other shoppers wait patiently for a personal portion of their knowledge and hospitality, these women remain steadfast in genuine interest, eyes locked until I finish speaking. Much like a hair stylist, they are accustomed to exposing imperfections while practicing the fine art of counseling women through vulnerability, all while keeping a safe emotional distance.

Our interactions have become more than sales transactions. I can't shop anymore without seeing the way Jesus loves these women standing behind cosmetic counters.

They don't know it, but I've prayed through each of their hardships as they've revealed them to me in our mirror conversations. Dabbing my neck with foundation to match my skin tone, one of them spills about a brutal recurrence of cancer, walking through the stages of healing, wearing hats to cover the baldness. For another, I hear tales of a slow recovery process and new rhythms required after hospitalization for a heart problem. One wants to write a book and seeks insight about overcoming resistance.

"What does your husband do?" Galina inquires, randomly, like asking, "How are you doing?" It's the first time any of them have asked, and it seems they are all waiting for my answer. I hesitate to respond and my mind sifts quickly through a number of ways I could answer. It's that awkward moment when what you say next could open the door to exploring faith in Christ or slam it closed. I inhale deeply to unleash bravery.

"My husband is a pastor—the equivalent of a CEO—for a church-planting movement in North America." I say it quickly, my cheeks flushing, waiting for affirmation in their facial expressions.

H is an Anglican priest. The formal title in front of his name reads, *The Venerable*. *Pastor* and *CEO*, while accurate descriptions of his job, are titles rarely used in the Anglican context. But in this scenario, they seem appropriate. One of the cosmetic girls admits knowing very little about Jesus or religion. Another asks what I do in the church. I tell her that I don't *do* church anymore, I try to *be* the church to people.

For me, *doing* church is an illustration in slothful living—not laziness, but mindless busyness, something you check off on a list for your week. The heart can become detached, the ritual commonplace, like a child's piece of art hanging on your refrigerator for months. Initially, it takes the centerpiece of daily activity, but over time the beauty is overlooked, lost in the mundane. Celebrating faith can become a callous responsibility.

My answer caps a growing curiosity about that "something different" Galina was sensing in our tangential conversations about faith. In essence, I tell her I belong to a church community, but I value changing the artwork of my spiritual life often because my soul needs fresh perspective. My business card reveals I am a storyteller of the beauty in redemption. That little tidbit, along with my husband's job title, becomes the catalyst for an *aha* moment in high definition. We embrace in the middle of the perfume aisle.

Talking about Sabbath is a lot like sharing my faith. I talk about it often, but with hesitancy. Not because I am ashamed, but because Sabbath is a foreign language to the native tongue of a busy culture, a curious oddity in an overtired church. When I'm unsure about a person's spiritual history, I walk around the word *Sabbath* as if I'm tiptoeing around fresh paint. I don't want my passion about the outcomes of weekly rest to scar a friendship with someone who defines Sabbath with a brush of legalism. I wait for the paint to dry a little between conversations before spilling the layers of my experience.

I'm struck by how many times Jesus performs miracles and then asks people to keep it quiet. "Don't tell anyone," he charges the crowds who witness the healing of the deaf man with the speech impediment (Mark 7:34–36).

He enters a house and doesn't want anyone to know about it and then casts a demon out of a woman's daughter (7:24). The disciples are charged to refrain from speaking about his transfiguration (9:9), yet he instructs the man freed from the legion of demons to "Go home to your own people and tell them how much the Lord has done for you" (5:14–19).

In a world searching for purpose by proclaiming every thought, word, and deed on Instagram, Facebook, and Twitter, I remember that Jesus is discriminating about how he communicates.

When I like to know outcomes and insist on putting the personality of Jesus within the parameters of my experience, I remember that the way of faith isn't a formula to follow but an intimate relationship of meaningful conversation. There is a reason why he permits sharing your heart sometimes and quiet pondering at others, why he says, "Wisdom is proved right by her deeds" (Matthew 11:19), not justified by the approval of others.

In the same way our history influences the perceptions we have about faith, the way we view the fourth commandment comes with an array of baggage—and sometimes an empty suitcase. In my case, ignorance is bliss. I was schooled well in the other nine commandments, by both the reverse mentoring of my alcoholic single mother and positive reinforcement in routine visits with my stable grandparents. But the riches of Sabbath remained a mystery, something I didn't think much about or hear preached from pulpits. What stands out most is this: The day we chose to rest was noticeably different than the other six, every weekend of my childhood.

Inhaling the fragrance of God's goodness in sacramental oils of a Catholic Mass remind me of routine weekend visits with my grandparents, tucked between them on a hard pew in the early years of my adolescence.

Distracted by families flooding down the center aisle of the church, traffic bottlenecks as each collared shirt and modest skirt take turns bowing toward the altar. Holding on to the end of the pew, each person wisps the sign of the cross over their chest. Hinges on kneelers crack open the hollow stillness, unfolding permission for tight young shoulders to slump and fidget.

Beyond bowed heads and elbows positioned like tent pegs resting on the backs of pews, I raise my eyebrows and cover up an uncontrollable grin when I see a gold chalice draped in white linen, the centerpiece of the altar with smudges of my fingerprints hidden beneath the cloth.

The day before, my grandmother filled the silent void in the sanctuary as she flipped the silver switch on the vacuum. Dragging the long cord in one hand at her hip, she pushed the beating brushes beneath the red velvet chairs where the altar boys and priests sit. I left the scent of Old English permeating the fibers of my dusting cloth, tiptoed past the open gates of the Communion rails, and satiated my growing curiosity. I wanted a small glimpse—to experience the vantage point of holiness.

Gliding slowly around each corner, I inherited a binocular view of the sacred accoutrements normally seen from a safe distance. I wiped my hands gently over the surface of the Communion table, tracing with my index finger the wood crevices of the Latin words carved into the frontal piece, and then perched myself gently on the velvet seats of the armchairs like a china doll swinging her legs over the edge of the top shelf. As I gazed out over the countless rows of empty pews, the veil between holiness and humanity was rent. God became real to me under the roar of the Hoover.

Church is something I only share with my grandparents. Dinner at the Flaming Pit, thick bakery cheesecake, *The Carol Burnett Show*, and Saturday-afternoon Mass are staples in our weekend routine. Grandma and Grandpa teach me how to fly a kite, swim, and ride a bike, memorize the Lord's Prayer, and believe in the power of bedtime prayer, that friendship in marriage is possible, and that coffee grounds are better for growing large roses and plump tomatoes. My loving grandparents gave me my first glimpse of the rhythms of Sabbath, assuring me it doesn't matter where you go to church, as long as you go somewhere.

Routines and rote prayers may seem boring, rigid, and lifeless. Oblivious to the tracks laid down by our parents and loved ones, we can easily miss the way those rhythms have become a steadiness in the chug of life until unexpected whistles blow, warning of danger on the journey as we know it. In the deep ravines of pain and suffering, repetition prevents derailing when going through dark periods. For you, it may be memorized prayers and Bible verses; for your neighbor, bedtime rituals with children that include thank-you prayers, or baking chocolate chip cookies on Friday in preparation for playtime on the weekend.

For several months of weekends, I memorized more than stained glass. I sat next to Grandma on the stiff tufted couch in their living room reserved for card parties and guests. She quizzed me from the catechism, practicing for answers I'd need to know for the verbal test the priest administered. One day he visited, and in that same room casually asked me questions from an armchair over afternoon cocktails and mixed nuts. It was a test I knew I'd flunk, yet it was graded on the curve of my nervous shyness and blushing cheeks of holy awe over the man who spoke intimately of God while seated in my grandparents' living room.

And perhaps those moments of grace were why I understood the pretend kindness between two broken people in my parents, who didn't have the right answers to marital success. Why I could stand at the altar and hold out my cupped hands, accepting Christ's body and blood, and not feel like a fake. Perhaps that's why I could understand unconditional love yet have a hard time accepting it for myself. And why I now understand as an adult that Sabbath may be blacklisted for some who experienced it as a day of "shalt nots" and believe that perspectives are altered beautifully by time and redemption.

I learned about the true face of love through the rhythm of predictable visits with my grandparents. It looks like Grandma's wrinkled hands folded over the prayer book in her lap as she was seated in the same chair every morning I woke up at their house. Her startled upward glance instigated by the sound of my footsteps was followed by an immediate smile every time our eyes met. Love resides in Grandpa's morning rituals, his buckled shoes shuffling an impromptu tap dance on the tile floor the moment he spies me in the small pink nightgown drifting across the kitchen. He twirls a dancing spatula to make me laugh. And every Saturday, he flipped Hungry Jack pancakes on the griddle because he knew they were my favorite.

Even when Grandma suffered with dementia, the Lord's Prayer and the Nicene Creed rolled off her tongue without a second thought, yet a tube of toothpaste and a toothbrush on the bathroom sink became a daily catalyst for conundrum. "What do I do with these?" she'd ask dumbfounded, childlike.

Our soul remembers what the mind easily forgets. What we pour into our soul today may seem inconsequential, yet it will provide a stabilizing anchor for the future. But when our anchor is made of the false material of legalism, freedom is stuck on the bedrock of false teaching.

My grandparents were never concerned about having all the right answers or impressing a priest. Communion was never as much about knowing information as knowing the Truth. Looking back, I realize that as the child of an alcoholic who rehearsed brokenness during the week, a consistent rhythm with my grandparents on the weekends meant I experienced Sabbath as a weekly restoration—a reminder that I was accepted not for what I did but for who I was when shame attempted to convince me otherwise.

As I grew into adulthood, weekends became workdays and a rhythm of Saturday phone calls to my grandparents replaced being with them. On the floor of my bedroom, using the wall as a headboard, I dialed the phone number I memorized the first time I used it as a child. Before the day became a rushing river of activity, carrying me away with it, I faithfully connected with the people who loved me relentlessly. While waiting for the familiar voice to echo through the line, the muscles in my shoulders relaxed, marking the beginning of the Sabbath I practiced during my childhood.

Until my grandparents breathed their last, no matter what was happening in my life, on Saturday I always stopped to make the phone call because my relationship with them mattered. Our weekly conversations were a priority that never varied with marriage or becoming a parent. When the phone rang on Saturday, they knew who was calling. And one of the greatest compliments I ever received in my life came during one of those calls.

"You are the best friend we've ever had," Grandpa said with deep conviction. My eyes misted in humble appreciation. The moment seemed sacred and is etched in my memory.

Abraham Joshua Heschel, Polish-born American rabbi and leading Jewish theologian, writes about Sabbath, using marriage as a metaphor for the way we love, honor, and cherish time with the Creator:

> About the middle of the third century, distinguished scholars speak of the seventh day not as if referring to abstract time, elusive and constantly passing us by. The day was a living presence, and when it arrived they felt as if a guest had come to see them. And, surely, a guest who comes to call in friendship or respect must be given a welcome. It is, indeed, told of Rabbi Yannai (a Jewish sage) that his custom was to don his robes on the eve of Sabbath, and then address himself to the ethereal guest: "Come, O Bride; Come, O Bride."[1]

My grandparents always treated me as if I was special, and Sabbath became an expression of our time together as different.

After Grandpa's death, despite her dementia, Grandma recognized my voice on the phone. Life-giving rhythms leave an everlasting imprint. While my grandparents have danced in heaven for some twenty years now, I still think about them every Saturday.

Their lives left an indelible legacy, informing the way I practice Sabbath now.

Belonging comes first; then belief follows. It is through the sacrament of presence and life-giving words that a hard heart becomes open and receptive. In childhood, Sabbaths with my grandparents were smudged with pancake batter, cherry cheesecake, and wet kisses. They weren't based on an agenda or specific desired outcomes, which cause so many people to struggle with Sabbath-keeping. Legalism has crushed the spirit of love and freedom God intended when he wrote the word *Remember* just before the word *Sabbath* on those stone tablets.

For many, remembering the Sabbath seems legalistic—one of the Ten Commandments, but extremely old-school—Old Testament-thinking, perhaps even a bitter recall of not being able to watch TV or laughing too loud with your siblings on that day.

Maybe your experience was similar.

Cathy wrote to me:

I grew up with the Ten Commandments preached and lots of fear induced about breaking them. I always felt that if I disappointed my parents then I disappointed the church and God. That is a lot to carry on one's back at any age, but especially as a child. Mostly, I feel like my childhood was full of misunderstanding about a day meant to be so special.

The Sabbath meant staying dressed up all day and just sitting around the house. We could watch TV and go outside but not to do anything fun. For some reason, my parents decided that going out to places like restaurants and movies was breaking the commandment. For them, that meant we were making people work on the Lord's Day. It was as if they thought they would be judged by God for enjoying a meal out because someone made the meal for them and got paid for it.

My dad forced me to wear high heels to church once I turned fourteen years old. To him, you were not dressed up for the Lord if you did not wear high heels. He was obsessed with and controlling about being dressed up and this greatly influenced my misunderstanding about the Sabbath.

In households where rest is a spiritual straitjacket for sanctification, Sabbath conjures a dreaded quiet day of doldrums or a set of rules for justification. The intent and truth of the Ten Commandments stand independent of time, shifting culture, and changing circumstances. God's authority is complete, perfect, and unchangeable, which means nothing can be added, taken away, or edited regarding his intention about Sabbath. People often ask me *how* to Sabbath before understanding *why* God made the Sabbath in the first place. This is like accepting a dinner invitation with friends based only on the menu. How hurt they would be if you chose not to accept because your options elsewhere seemed better suited to your palate. Jesus extends an invitation to resist working one day a week for deepening relationship and protection from influences that pull us away from him. He gave the Sabbath in great love, knowing the weekly union will satiate a deep hunger for belonging.

When we abide in Jesus, all our questions about *how* we Sabbath are answered in *who* we worship. How we Sabbath, though important, becomes a lower priority. What begins as a sacrifice of time becomes a willing surrender the more we choose it. We long for rest, and the Lord of the Sabbath longs for communion with us.

God is less interested in how we spend our Sabbath than that he has our undivided attention. More than our effort to separate a specific day of the week for rest, God longs for our presence with him. God wants our trust and relinquishment more than any other desired outcome. More than what we do for him, he longs for us to be with him, to trust he is working all things together for our good.

Once Cathy married and began exploring Scriptures for herself, the confusing messages about the fourth commandment she learned as a child converted into a clear message of refreshment, rejuvenating her faith:

I found that as my family refueled on Sabbath, people commented that they enjoyed being around us. I like to think we were a breath of fresh air for them. When friends ask questions about how we are able to rest, it provides opportunity for good discussions. I have noticed that if people want to incorporate Sabbath into their lives, they assume rules are necessary. I always share our story of simply finding a way to rest that works for us, and sometimes that means taking a rest from rules too. Sabbath is a lifestyle change not a day of change.

I believe it is of great significance that God begins the fourth commandment with the word *remember,* and also that he uses more words to convey this commandment than he does the other nine:

> Remember the Sabbath day by keeping it holy. Six days you shall labor and do all your work, but the seventh day is a Sabbath to the Lord your God. On it you shall not do any work, neither you, nor your son or daughter, nor your male or female servant, nor your animals, nor any foreigner residing in your towns. For in six days the Lord made the heavens and the earth, the sea, and all that is in them, but he rested on the seventh day. Therefore the Lord blessed the Sabbath day and made it holy.
>
> Exodus 20:8–11

He knows how easy it will be for us to forget that the Sabbath was created for us and not we for the Sabbath (Mark 2:27).

In Christ, Sabbath is a personal invitation for restoration and recreation uniquely fashioned for each of us. If we are called to be separate from the world and different from the norms society dictates, Sabbath communicates that difference to the people around us.

H and I pull into the garage after a night out with friends. Entering the house from the garage, we open the door into the kitchen and scan the room, searching for signs of our two children. Instead, I become distracted by the half pizza on the cutting board, now cold and rock hard. Dirty dishes fill the sink. I pull the scarf from around my neck, flip high heels from my feet to the corner, and begin unloading the dishwasher. Inside, resentment is building like a locomotive gaining momentum. With each plate and glass stacked in the cabinet, I threaten to blow off steam. *Why does everyone depend on me to clean up after them?*

As I plunge the greasy skillet into soapy dishwater, H walks into the room after changing into sweats. He sets another dirty glass from the bedroom on the counter. When we make eye contact, he asks, "What's wrong?"

"I don't really want to be doing dishes at 10 p.m.," I fume.

"Why aren't the kids doing the dishes?" he asks in rebuttal.

Murielle giggled at the movie she was watching from under a blanket on the couch. Harrison had just settled back into his bedroom after folding a load of laundry. The truth? I didn't want to impose. I didn't want to ask them to help. I hadn't set any boundaries for keeping them accountable regarding cleaning up after themselves and the result fueled anger and resentment.

When we choose to rest from work, it is an act of compassion toward ourselves. But if we are resentful, it is impossible to practice compassion. Resentment keeps us from resting. Do you often help others, but rarely, if ever, admit you need help? If your answer is yes, you may be deriving a false sense of self-worth. In order to feel a genuine sense of belonging, we must first believe we are worthy of love. We attempt to convince ourselves that our value is wrapped up in the measure of our busyness. "I'll be worthy when . . . I finish that project . . . clean the house . . . volunteer at church . . . [fill in the blank]." Sabbath reminds us that we are loved deeply and we belong to him. If we believe we are worthy just as we are—in yoga pants, three-day hair, and without makeup in a room that looks like a cyclone hit—rest comes easy. Those who Sabbath well usually exhibit self-acceptance.

Shame is the fear of being unlovable, and when we live as if we are unlovable, that mindset becomes a stumbling block to those around us. Choosing rest is the practice of loving yourself. You must become compassionate toward yourself first in order to become compassionate toward those around you. In the same way we cannot earn worthiness, we cannot earn a Sabbath heart. God gave us Sabbath as a commandment, not so we could achieve his love, but to show us how deeply he already loves us.

Jesus asks,

> Are you tired? Worn out? Burned out on religion? Come to me.
> Get away with me and you'll recover your life. I'll show you how
> to take a real rest. Walk with me and work with me—watch how
> I do it. Learn the unforced rhythms of grace. I won't lay anything
> heavy or ill-fitting on you. Keep company with me and you'll learn
> to live freely and lightly.
>
> Matthew 11:28–30 MSG

Week by week, as we take baby steps toward making rest a weekly rhythm, many begin recognizing the myths they've believed wrongly about Sabbath.

Sabbath is a long period of stillness and quiet to read, pray, and nap. If my current life situation doesn't afford that lavish gift, then I am exempt from Sabbath.

Sabbath is only possible after I get everything done.

Sabbath is only for those who are spiritually mature.

Sabbath can only be observed on Sunday. And because I have Sunday responsibilities, Sabbath is impossible for me.

Sabbath is something I do in order to become more productive.

Can you identify with some of these myths?

During a routine visit with my doctor, our conversation revealed she believed some of those myths about Sabbath. My doctor is my age and we talk like girlfriends sitting in lounge chairs on the beach. Repeating stats from some routine blood work, she commented that my cortisol levels were good and also that my blood pressure was perfect.

"Your stress levels look low," she commented.

"Yeah, I don't have a lot of stress in my life at the moment," I gushed.

She peered over her computer screen, arched her eyebrows, and paused for a moment. "I don't hear people say that often. I mean, maybe never."

My physician admitted she is stressed out, to which I quickly empathized, "Well, I'm not a doctor, and I do work from home." And then I was bold with an admission about why I think my stress levels are low.

I told her about observing Sabbath and the way the Sabbath Society keeps me accountable. She responded as if I'd given up the secret on how to pick winning lottery numbers. Shortly afterward, she divulged that her mother is Jewish, and then went on to describe a typical Friday in Israel. "They run around all freakish preparing for Sabbath and then everything stops at sundown. It's unbelievable." The prohibition of electricity and driving vehicles might have been mentioned too. To which I replied, "Well, we aren't legalistic; we're talking about baby steps here."

And even though she is resigned about the reasons why she can't Sabbath, we both agreed that God probably knew what he was doing when he made the Sabbath a commandment. He knows how much we need rest and how hard it will be for us to actually do it.

The brief encounter with my doctor brought the realization about the level of difficulty people have in making allowances for rest, even for a few hours.

During times of rest, not only do I uncover untruths associated with Sabbath-keeping, I also recognize the subtlety of myths I've believed about God. As I wait for answers about what I begin to discern is a call to London, the lies exposed sound something like this:

God's silence about my discontent in the place where I am living means he is ambivalent. What I'm asking for isn't important enough to garner his attention.

God's silence means I am unlovable and my prayers unimportant.

The way he will answer this prayer about living in London will look like the way he has answered each of eight transitions in the past.

Silence means I do not understand what he wants me to do.

The longer I wait, the more likely it is that I have lost the ability to discern his will.

He will answer my prayers after I have done my part. Because I am waiting, it means I've missed something important.

If I become impatient and doubt, his plans will be delayed or thwarted. Ultimately, I will have to wait longer due to a lack of trust.

Sabbath isn't another rung on a spiritual ladder we climb toward achieving smiles from heaven. No, it isn't what we do at all. God invites you to rest because he loves who you are. When you abide with him in Sabbath, an unshakable confidence shines from the inside out, enticing others toward the gift of rest as well.

Waiting for God to answer prayers isn't a spiritual game of chance. It's in the spiritual wilderness where we find God is working quietly on our behalf. In the silence, he is preparing all the details for what lies ahead. Sabbath is waiting for Christ to come into our everyday, messy, uncomfortable life and making sense of it all because he loves us.

In the same way I experience Galina's "something different about you" moment at the makeup counter and Cathy witnesses a change in the reaction of friends, we wear the welcome of Sabbath in our countenance. When his face is shining upon us, people notice the brightness, and Light dispels the myths.

CHAPTER FIVE

From How to Who

Sabbath is a time to transition from human doings to human beings.

Matthew Sleeth, *24/6*

Stepping off the stage during a break, I walk to the front row, crouch down, and slip pages of speaking notes on the floor beneath my seat. Inhale, and make my way toward a crowd of strangers that I've been speaking to all morning; women in ministry crowded around a smorgasbord lunch. But before picking up cutlery and a plate, I notice the pastor's wife from the host church standing alone in the back of the sanctuary, staring up toward the vaulted ceiling. When I approach, she makes eye contact and stops me with a question.

"How do you rest on Sunday?"

From experience, I know there is more behind that simple question. It sounds something like this: *How do you organize your life practically in order to make Sabbath a reality on the busiest day of the week?*

It's the question I expect to hear every time I speak about Sabbath. But when it comes from ministry leaders, I know the question piques from a place of quiet desperation—a weariness that assumes inserting rest into an over-scheduled agenda is unrealistic, if not impossible. For those with ongoing Sunday responsibilities, Sabbath as a rhythm of life seems elusive, outdated, and irrelevant. Yet I see glimmers of hope in the faces of those asking the question. Hope that I might have a magic answer they haven't discovered yet.

In twenty-five years as the wife of a minister, I can tell you I've pondered the same question, but only intentionally for the past three years of doing life together. What I discovered isn't a magic formula or five easy steps, but a way of life that changes how I and others make Sabbath a reality.

But before I tell you how Sabbath is possible for those challenged with Sunday responsibilities, ask yourself these questions:

When others point out your overtired state, is your response, "I'll rest when the work is done"?

Do you bemoan invitations for coffee or conversation?

Are you easily irritated by the needs of others?

Do you argue with family members on the way home from church because they insist on staying afterward to talk with people?

Do you plan ways of escape to avoid interacting with people?

Are you doing so much for God that you don't have time to be with him?

Imagine a sick day as a welcome retreat because at least you would have an excuse to rest without guilt?

Do you fear stopping because everything might crumble in your absence?

When you hear someone recite, "My yoke is easy and my burden is light," you assume the Bible verse is for everyone else. You think, Perhaps he forgot the footnote: with the exception of those in ministry.

It might surprise you to know that all of these questions aren't made-up scenarios, they are real-life examples—responses from faithful volunteers and ministry leaders in different places and circumstances of life. They are red flags that the time to stop is long overdue because their identity is slanted by their drivenness. Perhaps you can see yourself reflected in these questions.

"Sabbath is possible because of *setting* an intention about it—not just *having* an intention about it," explains Jan, a spiritual director who is passionate about soul care. She and her husband recently relocated to help plant a church, and she describes her role as unpaid staff, wearing multiple hats:

What works for me is scheduling time. I look for half days or entire days when I can unplug and rest and then guard that scheduled day by being firm about observing Sabbath. When I waffle by making exceptions, it's typically another two months before it happens again.

When there is Sabbath rest in my life, I find ministry springs forth from a spiritual place rather than a frantic, flesh-driven place. When I am not incorporating Sabbath, it is oh-so-easy to fall into people-pleasing and doing things for prideful or selfish motives rather than using spiritual discernment and seeking the Holy Spirit. Sabbath seems to keep things much more balanced regarding commitments and decisions in ministry—and life in general. This invariably even spills over into my marriage! Sabbath is an essential tool for "centering" in my life.

Creation is a story of continual new beginnings because God is in a constant state of creating, which leads me to tell you something radical and potentially disappointing, depending on your outlook: Nothing is ever finished.

You will never find that sweet spot of being completely done and caught up because God is in the business of creating, and his creation is thriving all around us with big results: In the trees budding overhead, birds chirping, babies crying, your stomach growling at high noon—all signs God fills the void and emptiness with what satiates the senses.

God's creation is a life-giving inhale for all of us, and Sabbath is the exhale. Without the exhale our breathing becomes shallow or nonexistent.

Think about that for a minute.

If you were to take a big gulp of air and then fear letting it go, what would be the outcome?

Well, the answer is obvious, isn't it?

Within the context of rhythms for our busy workaday lives, if we abuse time by neglecting to incorporate Sabbath into our week, eventually what is natural becomes burdensome, uncomfortable, disrupted. Over time, a lack of rest leads to a wilting capacity. What begins as a life calling, exploring uncharted destinations filled with adventure and vistas of influence, eventually folds in on itself as we encounter the inevitable storms of life.

Has it been a while since you've exhaled?

We all have reasons, and good ones, as to why rest remains elusive. But if we were to truly examine the truth, fear would often be found as the origin of our excuses. Yes, some excuses are beyond our control. But most of us, especially those in leadership, lack the inner permission to slow down and get help. The constant needs of others create a fear that stopping to rest might be the end of our livelihood or our ministry.

Rachel is a worship leader who also leads in other capacities in her church from time to time. As a young married twenty-something navigating the balance of career, ministry, and personal relationships, she admits that she finds rhythms challenging. Blaming a lack of consistent Sabbath-keeping on being displaced for nearly eight months while waiting for the purchase of a house to go through, she now finds weekends consumed with painting, moving, and settling. And then she shares a vulnerable admission. Rachel laments,

*But honestly, the house move is not the source of my lack
of rhythm, because I didn't have it before either. I am so
aware that each day there is a precious opportunity to just
be with the Lord, and most days I miss it. I pray throughout
the day and listen to Christian talk radio on the commute
to work, but I rarely just sit with the Word and my journal,
and that is the way I hear the Lord speak back to me most.
I'm feeling parched and desperate to hear his voice again.
I know exactly what I need to do, but there is always "one
more thing," until I collapse exhausted into bed. I whisper,
"Speak to you in the morning, Daddy" before I'm asleep!*

In *The War of Art*, Steven Pressfield writes, "The more important a call or action is to our soul's evolution, the more resistance
we will feel toward pursuing it."[1]

"Resistance is futile" is a common phrase made popular by
Star Trek.[2] But more than futile, resistance is the force wielding
fear in an attempt to deconstruct providence. Thankfully, Moses'
mother, Jochebed, didn't allow resistance a hint of influence when
it came to saving her son from death. Making a basket bed from
reeds and pitch were not the result of being gripped with fear or
living as a passive bystander (Exodus 2:1–10).

Pressfield defines resistance as "that destructive force inside
human nature that rises whenever we consider a tough, long-term
course of action that might do for us or others something that's
actually good."[3] Can you imagine a Bible without the stories of
Moses to buoy our faith? The parting of the Red Sea, the burning
bush, the Ten Commandments. How might those stories have been
rewritten had Jochebed allowed resistance to bully her?

Resistance takes an outward focus and traps it inward. It looks
like self-sabotage, self-deception, self-corruption, and self-reliance.
See the pattern here? Later, Moses faces his own war with resistance that begins with that four-letter word *self*. Self-doubt. He is
the traveling salesman carrying suitcases full of excuses.

When God tells Moses to lead the Israelites out of Egypt, Moses' first response is: "You want me to do what?"

"Who am I that I should go to Pharaoh and bring the Israelites out of Egypt?" (Exodus 3:11). Then he follows up with a list of what-ifs, the same way we often respond to Sabbath.

What if saying no to a lunch invitation hurts someone's feelings? What if neglecting housework leads to more work? What if taking time to rest results in people feeling neglected? Who will watch my kids? What will my in-laws think?

Sabbath is a life raft Jesus extends to us every week to prevent us from drowning in our work. It's not enough to know how to get to the other side of your busyness—it is doing something about it that will set you free.

Resistance is an outcome of self-reliance. And self-reliance almost always leads to self-doubt. And most all self-doubt is rooted in comparison, that fear of insignificance that petrifies.

And the thing about comparison? It's lying to you because it only reveals half the truth, which makes you think your resistance—self-doubt, self-reliance, self-sabotage—is the right response. Here's the thing: Sometimes we learn humility through the school of adversity, and that makes us distrust our qualifications.

It sounds something like this: "He knows how to Sabbath better because he's more experienced, more godly, more organized, more . . . [fill in the blank]" or, "The stage of her life makes Sabbath doable," as if what we need to do in order to get to a place where we can rest isn't normal or proper or valuable because it's not how someone else arrived there.

Can I tell you it doesn't matter? What Moses thought about himself or what others thought about Moses really didn't matter in God's grand perspective. He spoke, and that was all Moses needed for assurance; he was able, the right man for the job. It's the same for us who long for a Sabbath heart.

Before Moses is handed the stone tablets inscribed by God's finger, God informs Moses about all the ways he is setting him up for success. Skilled workers filled with the Holy Spirit make everything from the Tent of Meeting, table and lamp stands, every detail thought out, down to the anointing oil and utensils. And then he tells Moses to communicate this one last thing. A detail not to be missed:

"Say to the Israelites, 'You must observe my Sabbaths. This will be a sign between me and you for the generations to come, so you may know that I am the Lord, who makes you holy'" (Exodus 31:13).

Back then, resistance meant death, but in Christ, we are saved from the consequences of our foolish choices (Ephesians 2:4–5). Nonetheless, these words in the Old Testament still ring true. Observing Sabbath is a sign to people of all generations that Jesus is Lord, Light in the darkness, Hope for chronic weariness, because he is the only way to salvation. He is Lord of the Sabbath and Lord of our lives, and so we no longer have to be self-reliant. What if making a choice to rest is the new way of evangelism? Can you imagine the surprised looks on the faces of friends and strangers when we respond to the question "How are you?" with "I'm rested."

What if you began seeing resistance not as a fault, ailment, or negative intruder, but a sure sign that what you are about to do is filled with purpose that leads to transformation?

What if resistance is actually the neon sign on the road of your life, communicating, *"Get ready, I'm about to do something in your life that is bigger than the sum of your parts."* And in small print below, it might say, *"It's going to be scary, but fear not, I am with you. I am the beginning, middle, and end of your purpose."*

God responds to all of Moses' questions saturated in self-doubt with his own questions: "Who makes a person's mouth? Who decides whether people speak or don't speak? Hear or don't hear? See or don't see?" (see Exodus 4:11).

Pressfield writes, "Resistance has no strength of its own. Every ounce of juice it possesses comes from us. We feed it with power by our fear of it. Master that fear and we conquer resistance."[4]

In the same way Moses wrestled with God's belief in his gifts, the turning point in making Sabbath a rhythm is determined by what you do with resistance. Will you let fear of the unknown and the need for certainty keep you from rest? Or will you push past "self" vying for first place and trust him with your time, regardless of the outcome?

In the end, once Moses gave God all the reasons why he wasn't qualified as a leader, God relented, "Okay, okay, you can take Aaron with you for support; he's on his way here anyhow." I'm embellishing, but that's how I imagine it. Thankfully, Moses' story ends imperfectly brave and mightily heroic. In this I find solace, knowing perfection is never the goal of God's friendship with us.

> For the foolishness of God is wiser than men, and the weakness of God is stronger than men. For consider your calling, brothers: not many of you were wise according to worldly standards, not many were powerful, not many were of noble birth. But God chose what is foolish in the world to shame the wise; God chose what is weak in the world to shame the strong; God chose what is low and despised in the world, even things that are not, to bring to nothing things that are, so that no human being might boast in the presence of God
>
> 1 Corinthians 1:25–29 ESV

Imagine Jesus answering your *what if* questions regarding Sabbath doubts with the same questions he asks Job during a time of lament. Questions comprising three chapters, beginning with "Where were you when I laid the foundation of the earth? Tell me, if you have understanding. Who determined its measurements— surely you know!" (Job 38:4–5 ESV). Like a good coach, those weighty questions draw out the ways God is already at work in Job's life, putting any temptation toward resistance into proper perspective.

In the same way God asks questions, I ask Rachel, the worship leader, to ponder some too:

Why are you unwilling to risk stopping for rest?

Why do you lack faith in this commandment?

What could you be telling yourself that keeps you resistant toward Sabbath?

What are you afraid you might hear if you stop?

When I read those (hard) questions now, it's pure grace that she writes back with a *Thank you, Shelly,* and then makes a humble admission:

> *I'm pondering those questions, and while I feel there are some obvious answers for me, I suspect there are some deeper ones, as the ones I am currently holding onto don't outweigh my deep desire to build rhythm and rest. Given how long I have been wrestling with this, and how passionately I expound rest to those around me, I think there is possibly something left to uncover (or rediscover) that is stopping me from resting well. The irony? I haven't stopped long enough to ponder this really deeply.*
>
> *I suspect, as with most of life, it comes down to a need to be wanted/needed/useful/productive that comes out as busyness, and therefore my identity and security is not being centered fully in God.*
>
> *I know that this is going to be crucial for me to learn well now, to support whatever it is that I do going forward, and I'm constantly encouraged that he is faithful to work in me even when I'm not holding up my end of the deal!! He is good!*

One of the ways we quiet resistance to Sabbath-keeping is accountability. We encourage, speak honestly, and extend grace to one another. And remember that God made the Sabbath for us because of love—more love than we can possibly imagine. It's one of the reasons I started the Sabbath Society in the first place.

A few months later, Rachel writes to tell me how her Sabbath is progressing while continuing a commitment to Sunday responsibilities:

I feel like I'm breathing a different kind of air when I'm lead-
ing worship—like I'm alive in a way that God had in mind
when he made me—but it's also completely exhausting. I
give everything out and often feel spiritually, physically, and
emotionally drained afterward.

Rachel tells me she's been experimenting with splitting Sabbath
in two parts. On the weekends, when she fulfills a worship commitment, she plans something fun, restful, and nourishing on the
Saturday afternoon and evening beforehand. And after church on
Sunday, she makes an allowance for rest by saying no to socializing
over lunch. Of course, there are always exceptions when appropriate. Instead of a long lunch out, she spends time watching movies,
going for a walk, dipping into crafts, and enjoying some carbs to
make the day celebratory, different, and most of all, replenishing.

It means that I feel like I've had two significant blocks of rest,
with a slot of outpouring in the middle. I feel rested going
into Sunday morning, but I also know that I get to "crash"
after the service, and it gives me the emotional energy to
give everything I have while I'm leading. It doesn't matter if
I'm left empty, because I know I'm going to spend the rest
of the day filling up again!

Being creative with time, even by designing your own offbeat
rhythms of rest, is an integral part of Sabbath for many, especially
for those with regular Sunday responsibilities. Many report that
planning ahead—selecting recipes, checking the pantry, making
grocery lists, thinking through upcoming meetings and appoint-
ments, and saying no to some good invitations is worth the effort.
Preparation preserves peace, not just for those who lead but for
the way intentional rest translates into healthy ministry:

When I'm resting regularly, I see God's hand in my life as a
sign of grace. When I am not resting, I start seeing it as a

divine pat on the back. It makes me feel good about myself,
but then comes the pressure to keep it up. We get burnt out
when we are trying to control things that are too big for us
rather than keeping obedient in the daily and weekly "small
things."

If we only make choices that are linear cause and effect, without realizing the benefit of self-enrichment, or believe that our joy and delight somehow robs the poor and suffering, what we communicate to people is service or ministry that is dreary, obligatory, and painful. And who wants to follow that?

If you are a leader, whether on a grand scale or within the small group of people living under your roof, you must be compassionate to yourself first before you can be compassionate to others. When was the last time you were compassionate to yourself? When was the last time you chose to "waste time" by doing something pleasurable without guilt?

I am championing rhythm, fighting for it despite daily interruptions and changes swirling all around us. Rhythms enhanced by self-compassion keep us steady and paddling forward when we feel off-balance, like standing up in a rowboat on choppy water. We can attempt to throw out a life raft to the world around us and lead people back toward safety through discipleship, but anchoring time that is set apart and holy is much more challenging, isn't it?

How do we create time that is sacred in Sabbath-keeping? We make it different from the other six days of the week. The Sabbath remains holy even when we don't choose to observe it. Here are a few places to begin:

Create whitespace by carving out a time period for rest that becomes a weekly rhythm. If one entire twenty-four-hour period seems like a monumental feat, dedicate the first hour of your day off to rest, reflect, and abide in God's presence before taking a shower, cleaning up breakfast dishes, or starting DIY projects. I have a hunch that one hour will stretch once you experience the benefits of peace.

Many with ongoing Sunday commitments make rest a priority on another day of the week. And this is different from a day off for leisure activity. Sabbath is a time with heightened awareness of God's nearness, his presence with you. An expectancy and longing for intimacy in relationship like a couple who has been separated anticipating reunion.

The key to successful rest periods is preparing for him to come. Walk toward Sabbath instead of away from it. Make meal plans, shop, and run errands ahead of time and find yourself anticipating the joy of an extended period sans household duties. We'll talk more about this in future chapters.

In *The Right to Write*, Julia Cameron encourages a weekly artist's date to fuel inspiration for writers.[5] The practice offers the same result for any of us. Take a day trip somewhere new, stop by an art gallery on a daily commute, visit a state park with a camera, or peruse a local farmers market to cultivate rejuvenation and refreshment. Taking a break from regular routines, whether walking a different path or driving a new route, widens perspective and inspires creativity, circumventing ministry ruts we are apt to fall into.

Keep your phone and laptop turned off for the time set apart for Sabbath. Eliminating distractions and creating boundaries with those in your spheres of influence provides an atmosphere of healthy respect that becomes surprisingly contagious. In the early years of ministry, before cell phones, H and I didn't respond to phone calls or impromptu visits on our days off. And people honored the boundary. When the word *emergency* is clearly defined by you and your dependents, practicing this discipline becomes easier.

If you enjoy reading, take a break from self-help or work topics and read a novel instead. If you normally take notes for work projects, talks, or blog posts on your computer, jot down your thoughts in a journal. The discovery of what pours out might surprise you when the paragraphs aren't attached to productivity.

Sabbath is about celebrating the goodness of our Creator. Stand back like an artist looking at his masterpiece from a distance, and you'll notice the gradations of color and vibrancy in life formerly missed in your busyness. Laugh, play, watch a movie, and give yourself permission for feasting. Enjoy food and drink that you normally don't allow yourself during the other six days of the week. Sipping a favorite tea, savoring a favorite food, or popping open a bottle of champagne on the day you choose Sabbath can make the time feel different, special, other than.

The grace of small Sabbaths throughout the week provides soul care for spiritual leaders, especially in seasons of spiritual winter. When suffering through loneliness of heart or the pain of disappointment, rhythm becomes a saving grace in the wilderness. At the same time, rhythms of rest provide preparation for busyness inherent in seasons of spiritual springtime.

When I answered the pastor's wife's question at a clergy spouse retreat about how I rest on Sundays, I told her that I begin Sabbath on Saturday at sundown. I use paper plates, leave any dishes used in the sink, laundry unfolded in a heap, and turn off the computer. I make a Crock-Pot meal and plan to eat leftovers on Sunday.

In silence, she nodded, then made eye contact. "What I'm hearing you say is that being fully present with people is a priority." Processing my answer to her "how" question became an unintended realization: A hurried-up-on-the-inside approach to Sunday morning worship results in scattered and rushed responses to people who are looking for guidance and empathy.

Rhythms look different for all of us and yet harmonize beautifully in community. I saw this lived out while speaking to another group of women in Phoenix, Arizona.

Finding the middle place in the dim room among round tables draped in white cloths, I stand under a ceiling of twinkling lights and speak to a diverse group of women. They're gathered in a small space in an urban church, at tables with china teacups and pretty plates of cookies. Desert Mission Anglican Church has asked me to tell them about the Sabbath Society.

A few dozen familiar faces from my spiritual history are in the audience and long to hear about my kids, whom they watched grow into adolescents. They want to know about the ministries we are leading. As I share about the weekly email I send to a growing group who observe a rhythm of rest instead of something that suits convenience, my eyes shift to my friend Barbara, the pastor's wife. She is leaning over her teacup held with both hands, her mouth slack. A handful of volunteers have the same expression. Pausing, I know what their blank stares communicate, just like I knew the last time I spoke to ministry leaders.

How do you do it? How do you Sabbath?

Barbara is not only a pastor's wife of a new church plant in Phoenix but also a full-time legal assistant for a very large company. She describes church planting as "a challenging task; the cement is so wet. No guidelines, programs, history, facility, or money! To say that Sabbath has not existed for me is an understatement," she admits.

It turns out that those natural gifts in administration and hospitality that make her successful at work are also the assets needed to grow a new faith community. She is in high demand, and like most things in life, our greatest strengths can also become points of weakness in self-reliance. She describes herself as a firstborn natural overachiever who believes a supernatural strength has carried her through years of constant nonstop activity.

I host an online book club using Dr. Matthew Sleeth's *24/6: A Prescription for a Happier, Healthier Life,* and Barbara joins us by purchasing the book. Inspired by the content, she passes the book on to her husband when our time together is finished. She writes to tell me what happened:

John was so moved by the realization of our 24/7-culture that his sermon on Sunday at Desert Mission centered on Sabbath. The epistle reading was about Jesus feeding the five thousand, and John chose to highlight the point of Jesus' need to withdraw, to be alone with the Father to process the

*things that were happening. Things were very quiet in the
church. I could feel the Holy Spirit hovering over the group
as they heard these words and pondered how they too could
incorporate Sabbath rest.*

Reading a book about the results of an overtired culture from
a doctor's viewpoint was a push in a stack of opportunities lined
up to create a domino effect of Sabbath-keeping among members
in the church.

Later, Barbara sent another email, letting me know they are
beginning a personal Sabbath rhythm with a family dinner in their
home on Friday—an intentional stop on work until sundown on
Saturday, with the exception of John's prearranged meeting with
church leadership. During that meeting, John discusses the Sabbath
focus from his sermon, and a decision is made by the leadership
team that he will share more about rest in sermons over the coming weeks.

Barbara writes,

*As I encounter the thought of intentional Sabbath while
participating in the book club, I realize how I have tried to
run fast to accomplish what I thought was important. A lot
of work has been done—admirable things; lovely times of
fellowship, spiritual growth; history has been written, programs are defined, facilities are made available. But now that
the cement has dried a little and we can actually walk on it, I
look forward to just sitting down with a book, a candle, and
a few friends to contemplate what the frenzy was all about.
I want to listen for his plan for the next steps. I anxiously
await the outcome!*

*Thanks to you, Shelly! You have stirred up something
here in Phoenix for sure. I am so glad you were able to
spend a little time with our ladies while you were in town.
Sabbath Revival? Let's take back what the devil has stolen
from us.*

Choosing to leave work undone for rest isn't a sign of weakness and failure. On the contrary, choosing rest over work is the ultimate act of brave trust in God's sovereign hand upon creation. He is in charge of our minutes.

From ministry leaders in the Sabbath Society there comes a *sacred echo* from intentional weekly rest.[6] Ministry springing forth from a place of peace fuels a heightened awareness of God's presence with us. A renewal of sensitivity to the Holy Spirit informs leadership decisions with great results. Without Sabbath, it is easier to fall into people-pleasing and making decisions based on selfish motives, not only in volunteerism and ministry vocation but also in core relationships.

Ultimately, an acute awareness of God's voice resounds through busyness and transforms what we do in work into an everyday state of being, rooted in confidence as his beloved children. Sabbath as a rhythm of life changes the questions of life from *how* to *who*.

Sabbath is a weekly reminder that God cares more about who you are than what you do.

CHAPTER SIX

Stop or Be Forced to Stop

If we do not allow for a rhythm of rest in our overly busy lives, illness becomes our Sabbath—our pneumonia, our cancer, our heart attack, our accidents create Sabbath for us.

Wayne Muller, *Sabbath*

I am as certain of some things as I am about the lines on my face. But on most days, I have more questions than answers.

Crouching down in the opening underneath the bathroom sink, I scour through hair spray, brushes, and cosmetics, looking for a curling iron, when a still, small voice wisps through my thoughts and slows down my pace. Some people call it premonition or coincidence, but I like to think it's a love letter sliding through a crack in my busyness.

I hear Jesus whisper, *"I'm dictating a forced rest. The unplanned vacant space seated in a doctor's reception area or during a train commute; while you are seated in an airport terminal or strapped in for a road trip; these are armchair altars for cultivating relationship with me. I'm creating windows of time for the overflow of your life to spill out and become a love offering. Trust me.*"

I had phoned the pediatrician moments earlier about my daughter with a reply from the receptionist, "Can you be here in an hour?" I was still wearing pajama pants and bedhead. The last time I drove her to a doctor's appointment, she didn't have a license in her wallet yet. I hesitated about making the appointment because a mother knows her child's quirks like the smell of milk after the expiration date. Murielle has a history with sore throats, but her father insisted. So we went.

"I can't remember the last time you had strep," I tell Murielle, flipping through a magazine from the chair in the corner of the patient room, my voice echoing off sterile walls and the cold tile floor. Her legs dangle over the edge of the examination table, paper crinkling underneath. This kind of sore throat almost always brings back memories of an awful season in her childhood.

First grade. It was the year of the recurring strep infections, so many her pediatrician threatened to remove her tonsils if she got one more within a month. Two months passed, an embarrassment of riches.

"I don't think I have strep," she announces, kicking her feet against the table. "My throat isn't as painful as I remember it being during those years when I had them so often. But maybe my memory isn't accurate."

"I know," I say. "Sometimes our memory distorts reality. Like the time I visited my childhood neighborhood and realized the wealthy homes I envisioned as monstrously large were actually quite average."

"Yeah, and that time at our church, before we lived here, when I got separated from you and Dad," she rambles, "all I remember is how huge the campus seemed and how all I saw when I was frantically trying to find you was a sea of legs like a forest of tree trunks."

"I don't remember that," I chuckle with my hand cupped over my mouth.

Laughter made breathing more difficult through her stuffy nose. "Of course you don't remember, you weren't the one living it," she scoffs.

A nurse—holding a thermometer and the anticipated long wooden swab to sample the back of her throat—walked into the room, interrupting our laughter. Chatter diminishes under the clipboard holding my daughter's medical history, and I think about how memory is a distorted mirror of thinking when using it to reflect into the future.

"Negative," said the nurse as she peeked around the doorframe a few minutes later. "All your tests are negative. You have a virus that must run its course."

"I thought so," I said, nodding with Murielle.

Those who are sick live with a mixture of deep sadness and relief. And though I'm not currently in this category of life, I can understand this curious juxtaposition. Have you ever been forced to stop because of sickness and found relief in the excuse to rest?

Even though Murielle was feeling miserable, head stuffy and body weary, I witnessed a return to her true self during those days of slow recovery on our living room couch. All the stress of her outer world fell off, allowing what mattered most in the heart to surface, for both of us. Under blankets and pillows, lying in the center of our home, those days of lingering in rest and quiet opened a window to the sacrament of presence. Moments of meaningful conversation between us still echo.

After that appointment with the doctor, we climbed back into the car, stopping at Chick-fil-A for a milkshake on the way home. As she slurped chocolate through a straw, Murielle coached me by asking good questions. She knew I was struggling to find resolution in an important situation.

And like any successful coaching process, clarity comes quickly when I hear the answers to her questions pour out of my mouth.

"Mom, maybe I stayed home today to help you find the answer," she tells me with predictable insight beyond her years.

"Yes, honey, maybe so."

The resolve to make Sabbath a rhythm of life can take a U-turn as soon as we encounter inevitable disruptions. The unexpected, unplanned interruptions of life wave us back to the familiar, patting the couch cushions. Soon, we avoid rhythms altogether. But in these moments of disorientation, we have a choice. We can interpret interruptions as roadblocks to peace or as moments for deepening relationship, trusting in the path God dictates. We are never stuck in our circumstances; we are stuck when a mindset keeps us trapped in small perspective. A forced Sabbath is a ruthless grace, pulling us out of danger in order to move forward at a slower pace. The plans God has for us are unchangeable, but the way we get there changes in a forced Sabbath.

Realities often fall short of what we envision; let's just admit that. And when we assume outcomes depend solely on us, the body will eventually let us know that self-reliance isn't the answer for maximum health. Sabbath is preventive medicine; an intentional relinquishment before your body forces a complete stop.

The way toward arriving at a peaceful place of inner quiet isn't by creating unrealistic standards about miles logged, pages written, and widgets produced, but by fighting for the riches of rest with unwavering determination before mind, body, and soul impose a strike without your consent. Author Mark Buchanan says, "Determination grows best in the soul of pain,"[1] and if that is true, then making Sabbath a rhythm of life isn't for the faint of heart; it takes courage.

In the same way lament during Lent comes before the joy of Easter, finding a Sabbath rhythm can feel weighty and impractical until resurrection awakens us. The joy of Sabbath arrives when we believe it is a gift available for everyone regardless of situation. May we be people who recognize that disorientation isn't a negative, but the beginning of a new way forward. Disorientation is the perfect storm reminding us how desperately we need a Savior, a remembrance that he is with us, always.

Admitting our brokenness is the best place to start. Author Alan Nelson says that one of the elements God uses in the breaking process is to get us to stop, or at least slow down long enough to evaluate our priorities and motivations:

> When the body experiences extreme hurt, it often goes into a state of shock. When our emotions are damaged, we experience a nervous breakdown. Both of these processes actually enable the organism to repair itself. Brokenness is a sort of speed bump in life. When we fail to slow down, we are likely to do some long-term damage to our lives.[2]

Murielle and I experienced this kind of brokenness Nelson writes about on another visit with a doctor. Only this time it wasn't a sore throat or a pediatrician's office. It was in the emergency room, and I didn't drive her there. I followed an ambulance.

◆ ◆ ◆

Jolted awake by the vibration of my phone on the nightstand, I grasp it off the charger and see by the numbers that Murielle is calling. I assume she is letting me know she's on her way home from a late showing of an anticipated movie premiere. It's the first time I've let her drive this late on a school night. Her license, tucked behind the plastic sleeve in her wallet, has only been there for eight months. When I look at the clock, I see it's 12:40 a.m., later than I thought. Normally, she would call her dad, but he's on a trip in Denver.

When I answer, I hear screaming through a garbled disharmony, "Mommy, I am so sorry, I'm so sorry." She's repeating the same phrase over and over and over again. That's when I wake up from the dream I thought I was having and join her nightmare.

I hold the phone away from my ear and look at her picture on the screen again to make sure the voice isn't a middle-of-the-night prank or a wrong number. Perhaps she has phoned me by mistake. Is that laughter I'm hearing? My ears ring with the familiar sound of her voice, but I can't understand the gravity of what she is saying. It's as if I'm piloting through complete cloud cover, dependent on the instruments of my experience. But I don't have any experience with this. Suddenly the voice of a stranger pours cold water over all of my senses and sobers me into action:

"I'm a nurse, and your daughter is okay," she says. "I'm staying with your daughter until emergency crews arrive."

"Wait a minute, what happened?" I ask. "Where is she? Where are you? Who is this?"

"Your daughter was just hit by an 18-wheeler near the grocery store—she is lucky to be alive. We're at the corner of Highway 17 and the Causeway; do you know where that is?"

"Yes, I'll be there in five minutes," I say, springing out of bed and throwing the phone on the mattress.

I trade pajamas for yoga pants lying over the vanity stool and robotically push my legs into them, willing my mind to think through details while my body remains in constant motion. I'm aware of the sacredness of seconds ticking. The once extravagant choices in my closet are now utilitarian options for navigating trauma. I walk out of the house and into the garage, holding the phone in my hand, car keys dangling from one finger, and stop on the first step. *Breathe.* Make sense of scrambled thinking. Leaving Harrison behind to sleep, I push the button on the garage door opener. Squeaky wheels crack open a haunting stillness in the neighborhood.

Streets are dark and vacant when I roll down the window, hoping the air slapping my face will provide brisk lucidity. As I pull onto the highway, blue flashing lights in the distance bounce off the silhouettes of tall pines standing at attention. I gasp for breath and dial H. Through the haze of my sleepiness, a moment of clarity surfaces as a question while I wait for him to answer. *Why is God allowing this to happen while H is sleeping in a hotel room in Denver? He handles thinking on his feet better than I do.*

As I approach the scene of the accident, recounting the call from our daughter to H, colored lights dance between emergency vehicles, blinding my vision and confusing my senses. I halt our conversation abruptly to focus. Circling to find an out-of-the-way parking place, I see the mangled mess of metal that was once the shiny hood of the Volvo she's driven for a few months. Engine fragments pulverized and strewn into a million tiny pieces sparkle over the road and into the median.

On foot, I find her sitting in the driver's seat, black boots resting on the pavement. An EMT crouches in front of her, strapping a brace around her neck and over a new sweater imprinted with rows of white swans. She notices my presence, tilts her watery eyes in my direction, and whispers the same phrase again, "I'm so sorry, Mommy."

Clutching her shoulder, I tell her not to be sorry. "You are alive and that's all that matters."

Nearby, a man wearing a metal fireman's hat with the strap hanging loose under his chin stands with eyes focused on a clipboard pressed into his chest. When I ask what happened, he looks up like I've startled him out of a trance. Words come out of his mouth, but my mind isn't making the connection. I struggle to comprehend what he's saying like watching still frames of frenzy on a muted movie. The only decipherable phrase from the paragraphs he is speaking to me is this: "It's a miracle she is alive."

I latch on to his broad arm, steadying a sudden onset of uncontrollable trembling. The gravity of what happened hits me. My daughter has narrowly escaped falling through the hole in the veil between heaven and earth. When I ask him to repeat how the accident happened, he says, "It doesn't matter. One more inch and this would be a different scenario. You don't want to go there; all you need to know is, she is a miracle."

As the ambulance pulls away, I crawl back inside my car, rest my forehead on the steering wheel, and shake like a washing machine off balance. I am thinking about who I can ask to hold my hand in the next scene of this horror flick. None of my family members live within driving distance. Whom do you call at 1:30 a.m. when you are alone in the shock of trauma?

Names begin scrolling through my mind, all of which have an attachment to the heartbreaking church split we have recently experienced. Still lingering in the recovery room of that aftermath, I hadn't felt this alone since the days of my adolescence, living with a single mother struggling with misplaced brokenness.

With hesitance, my trembling fingers click on the number of the single person who offered empathy during the events leading to the church split despite being on opposite sides of the church fence. Dina let me know our friendship is worth saving, but it's now the middle of the night and she doesn't answer. I close my eyes and ask God for help, then think and listen.

And this is what I hear him whisper back: *You often feel like you need someone else to handle the hard stuff, the stuff that overwhelms you, that you don't think you are capable of doing on your own. You think other people are more equipped than you. And I'm showing you, right now, that you can do this. Because I'm with you and I'm enough.*

Opening my eyes, I stare out the windshield and watch another fireman push a broom across the highway, heaping bits of metal and plastic from the front end of my daughter's car into the median. I exhale self-doubt, turn the key in the ignition, and call H back with an update. The drive to the trauma center—I know it is more than fulfilling a parental obligation that feels like climbing Mount Everest in sandals. This is a divine appointment with a choice attached.

Listening to the tender, logical voice of H coming through the speaker on my phone, I exchange the fear of vulnerability with courage, believing in myself.

An hour later, I walk into a quiet hospital room void of color, illuminated by fluorescence, and find her lying alone, strapped to a board on a table, head haloed by orange plastic, arms lying at her sides with thick needles attached to tubes sticking out in the bends. When I walk into her line of sight, grab on to her hand, and ask how she is feeling, she repeats the same phrase again with tears sliding down the side of her face: "I'm so sorry, Mommy."

She tells me that she is sorry that she woke me from sound sleep, sorry that she wrecked the car we sacrificed to purchase for her. Sorry she's kept me up all night to deal with complex details alone, without her father to navigate. Sorry that she wasn't more cautious when she made a mistake at the traffic light. She is sorry that her brother is alone in the house an hour from our presence, and she is guilt-ridden over the possibility of missing school tomorrow, because people are counting on her to participate in planned projects.

When I assume I need to understand outcomes before taking the first step, I pray that I will think of my daughter's knee-jerk reaction toward selflessness. Faith is no longer a reduction of my understanding of Christ but the way of awe and worship and obedience.

"I have to use the bathroom," Murielle says, and we both laugh. It's going to take a monumental effort to extract her from the contraption binding her body to the table. But a young man wearing teal scrubs hears our laughter in the doorway and assists in freeing her from the table.

An hour later, we pad quietly through the dim house to her dark bedroom. After she is tucked in, I sit on the edge of her bed and marvel over the miracle. God saved her life. Whispering sleepy prayers, we thank him that she and the other driver weren't badly injured, that the police officer who initially seemed gruff and emotionless didn't issue a ticket and shielded her driving record. We thanked God that her brother slept through all of it.

Back under the sheets of my own bed, I replay the events in my mind, moments of horror that turned into a marker of deeper trust. It started with answering the phone call every parent hopes they don't get, and the voice of a nurse I never encountered, though Murielle swears seeing her stand next to me at the scene of the accident.

I'm no longer afraid of tripping on the oversized pant legs of my indecision in moments of adversity. Faith stood the test in surrender. I met God on his terms, not my own.

There are two kinds of brokenness—voluntary and involuntary. Alan Nelson describes voluntary brokenness as the kind that allows God to do whatever he wants with us. Involuntary brokenness, on the other hand, comes as the uninvited guest of difficulty—divorce, job loss, death, chronic illness, the trauma of a car accident:

> You can choose one of three responses when involuntary brokenness comes your way. You can rebel and grow bitter. You can gradually give in under constant nagging and increased pressure. Or you can respond positively to it and mature. In essence, you can go through it, or you can grow through it.
>
> But when we go through difficult issues without developing an awareness of our inadequacies and God's love for us, we become broken in the wrong places.[3]

Nelson goes on to describe people broken in the wrong places as bitter, cynical, brittle, angry, and hateful; a shell of our former selves in old age. In essence, he is describing a person void of rest, but he is also describing someone who interprets long waiting seasons wrongly. A person like me.

Ten years of living with loneliness in the beautiful coastal south, I realize, isn't the result of God's absence but a divine interruption to peace so that expectation and hope can grow into the birthplace of calling. Instead of asking God, "Why?" I began to identify his voice in the midst of my inner turmoil. And what I found was clarity and loving-kindness. Living in expectation that life will be better is discovering what listening is to hopefulness. In expectant listening, we learn that God has not and will not forget about us. My unfulfilled longing for life as a Londoner became a hopeful future outlook the more I trusted in the silence.

I take comfort in Eugene Peterson's words when he says, "It wouldn't be the first time or the last time that a long period of seclusion sustained by providential hospitality was required to build the highways to Zion" (see Psalm 84:5) in a man or woman's heart.[4] Melville wrote that his isolating years on a whaling ship were my 'Harvard and Yale.'"

What if we translated a forced Sabbath—that point of relentless discomfort that comes with difficulty—as an opportunity to deepen intimacy with Jesus?

In our fast-paced, microwave, drive-thru world, we can miss the meaning of life blurring past when we avoid suffering and the ways God uses difficulty to re-route us. Romans says, "We can rejoice, too, when we run into problems and trials, for we know that they help us develop endurance. And endurance develops strength of character, and character strengthens our confident hope of salvation" (5:3–5 NLT).

I write to the Sabbath Society,

If you are in a season that overwhelms, can I encourage you not to give up and allow fear to bully you under the covers? Push through resistance; admit you need help creating new rhythms. Your vulnerable admission might provide a breakthrough, a resurrection that changes your life. I'm not hoping I'll get sick so I can rest. I don't wish that upon anyone. This is the point: God wants our attention no matter the circumstance. We must be willing to surrender.

I ask those in the Sabbath Society to reply to the email by describing their week. I'm surprised by what slides into my inbox. Words like *a haunting ending and fragile beginning, restless yet enlightening, reflective, forced,* and *anxious.*

Constance writes,

The "be anxious for nothing" kind, I am a cancer survivor. I had the dreaded four-month checkup scheduled for Tuesday, and lately I've been noticing a few unexplained aches and pains. As I sat in the oncologist's office, I was unusually chatty and unfocused. Fear had once again laid its grip on me and, being weary of all that lay behind me, I had done nothing to shake it off. So for weeks before the appointment, I was emotionally unavailable to my husband—scared—I was too busy thinking about me. Hoping I was wrong, but in my heart, expecting the worst.

Results? I'm fine. No signs of recurring cancer. But other test results indicate that this "forced Sabbath" has not made me stronger. I have not found rest. A healing of the body is not always a healing of the soul. Thank you for helping me to realize that. And I long for something more—true spiritual rest.

Overwhelmed by Constance's honesty, I write her back, declaring my thankfulness: "I thought about a friend whose husband had cancer and was walled up emotionally with fear. He didn't talk to her throughout the last days of his life. It was a wonderful lesson for me (painful for her, of course) about how fear destroys our essence. Your words, 'A healing of the body is not always a healing of the soul,' are profound and true. Praying that you will enter into his rest this weekend."

Constance writes back:

In practicing Sabbath rest, I'm reminded of the thought "Silence is the soul's oxygen." Although I am home alone in a very quiet house every day while my husband is at work, it seems oddly unquiet. My mind has been filled with worries and stress. As crazy as this now sounds to me, I even "borrow" my children's problems and worry about them. So I am hanging on to this thought. I am being quiet with these holy words: 'Be still, and know that I am God. My peace I give unto you, not as the world giveth, give I unto you' (Psalm 46:10; John 14:27). How good that peace is a continual giving; I need it every moment.

Constance reveals she is broken in the right places. She admits she doesn't have rest all figured out, but she is pressing in—learning, listening, abiding, believing God is the source of inner peace.

You may not have time for a whole day to rest, but a small window of time here and there cultivates a Sabbath heart. Pausing for prayerful listening, even for just a few minutes, brings everything that is important back into focus. We need whitespace for hearing the truth more clearly. Daniel Gross finds,

> In recent years researchers have highlighted the peculiar power of silence to calm our bodies, turn up the volume on our inner thoughts, and attune our connection to the world. Their findings begin where we might expect: with noise. The word *noise* comes from a Latin root meaning either "queasiness or pain."[5]

Read the headlines, talk to your neighbors, mentor a college student, and discover a similar truth: we experience pain, not as an exception, but rather as a normal part of our humanity. And the way to conquer pain is in finding Jesus' still, small voice above the noise.

Recent neuroscience research reveals that "freedom from noise and goal-directed tasks, it appears, unites the quiet without and within, allowing our conscious workspace to do its thing, to weave ourselves into the world, to discover where we fit in. That's the power of silence."[6]

Maybe you've just experienced a joyful holiday season punctuated with days of rest, and the thought of revisiting mundane practicality makes you feel tired, heavy, and lifeless. Perhaps you feel a bit guilty for feeling restless?

Florence Nightingale was on to something when she wrote, "Unnecessary noise is the most cruel absence of care that can be inflicted on the sick or well."[7]

When perspective becomes slanted and days are disoriented—when emotions are out of sorts and your heart feels heavy—rhythms reorient toward what matters most. Maybe you don't have the luxury of going somewhere quiet for long periods of reflection, but you can find a spot to sit and stare out the window while your kids are eating breakfast. In the same way you start your day with a predictable routine; incorporate three minutes a day to listen to your heart and hear what God is saying.

Natalie is the mother of three children, ranging in age from eleven to nineteen. She spends most of her time home-schooling the two youngest and enjoys being a wife and mother. As a faithful Sabbath Society member, Natalie proves she is learning to listen to her heart well, when she responds to that same email asking for one word to describe her week. She uses the word *right*.

My week was right. Even though my husband had to fly to North Carolina for two days, there was something every night, and I got stranded in the big city for several hours by an unexpected blizzard last night. The balance between crazy and cozy was right. In the midst of the craziness, the kids and I kept a Monopoly game going on the kitchen table. I had an outing with my oldest daughter, which revealed how much she'd matured since we did the same thing two months ago. Later, I even had a date and good conversation with my husband.

The idea of illness becoming our Sabbath, I think is so true. Sometimes a mild illness is a welcome break. On the other hand, sometimes waiting for our Shepherd to make us lie down is a cop-out.

By the time I sent out the next letter the following week, the weather, not sickness, inflicted a forced Sabbath. Three days of ice and snow in the tropical South erased everything scheduled on the calendar.

While I stood in long lines at the grocery store, preparing for what the weatherman was forecasting, my adrenaline pumped with anticipation. I witnessed a furious frenzy of frantic people removing the last loaves of bread from shelves and laughed (inside, not at them)—people moving at a frenetic pace over the potential lack of food, unable to frequent the places that serve fast food. I was excited about having an excuse to rest instead of worrying about a potential power outage.

Before our small patch on the world froze up and threatened to shatter into a million pieces, I dropped H's shirts off at the laundry. Never know when you might need a starched collar in the middle of a snowstorm, right?

The sullen Doonesbury behind the counter asked me, "How many?" straight up, like he changed his methods with the weather report. He always counts collars without making eye contact, hands me a yellow piece of paper with my husband's name (one letter) on it as if he's doing me a favor. His uncharacteristic question threw me off.

Walking back to my car, I passed a woman in a fur coat, with glasses resting on the end of her nose, carrying a pile of laundry. Her fancy red car was running with the door wide open. I guess she was in a hurry to buy bread across the street. *Only in a small town*, I thought. That car would have been gone in a skinny minute if this were New Jersey.

Driving across the street, I beat her to the store, helped the manager pack my groceries, and asked if she would be closing early. Lines of people were threading into each aisle, adults and children with armloads because the grocery carts were all in use. No one should risk crossing an icy bridge after nightfall, when the bread is already gone. The manager told me several customers and co-workers offered their couches if she became stranded. *Only in a small town.*

A rhythm of preparing for Sabbath, I realize, is similar to practicing for a natural disaster. Instead of being depleted, empty, and anxiety-ridden about what is ahead, I'm experiencing peace on the inside regularly, not just in calm circumstances.

Sabbath is a time set apart to learn about trust, available any day of the week, not just on Sunday. The outcome of being a faithful student of the process is supernatural peace. We are the natural and he is the super, a friend once told me. Jesus illustrates this best as he falls asleep on a rocking boat tossed about by violent wind. Fearing for their lives, the disciples wake him and Jesus responds, "Oh no, help!"?

Wrong. He tells them, "You of little faith, why are you so afraid?" (Matthew 8:26). Jesus calms the wind and waves with words of peace.

Honestly? The forced Sabbath imposed upon us by the weather gives permission for extended times of listening prayer. In hard spiritual winter seasons, like the one I am currently living, we need conversation with Jesus like we need food to keep from wilting.

When we think of Jesus, we think of him as doing things—praying, casting out demons, speaking to crowds, feeding throngs of hungry people, healing the sick. But he also disappeared a lot. He withdrew to a mountain, the wilderness, and even paddled out in the middle of a body of water to be alone and pray (Mark 1:35).

"When Jesus prayed he was at rest, nourished by the healing spirit that saturates those still, quiet places. . . . This can help us begin to understand one aspect of Sabbath time: a period of repose, when the mind settles gently in the heart," writes Wayne Muller.[8]

During a blizzard, we are tucked away for periods of repose that leave the mark of expectancy in otherwise anxious circumstances. Sabbath can only begin when we close the market on all the active pieces of our lives. Unexpected weather conditions allow a withdrawal from business as usual, filling our credit column with presence and taking photo opportunities with icicles. When we don't have the forced Sabbath of a snowstorm to slow us down, closing the market translates into turning off the computer, walking away from social networking, and letting go of writing, cooking, and the dishes for twenty-four hours.

"Better to have one handful with quietness than two handfuls with hard work and chasing the wind" (Ecclesiastes 4:6 NLT).

🍃🍃🍃

I trade the soup of my swirling thoughts for a cup of tomato crab with a hint of thyme, a lunch at a new-to-me restaurant with

Elizabeth, a friend with whom I share writing endeavors. Weary of yoga pants and pajamas, I long to wear cute jeans and boots and to breathe fresh perspective after being cooped up for days in my house.

We talk about author friends we have in common, our latest projects, celebrate publishing markers, and grieve the loss of a mutual friendship—a friend who chooses folly over truth as her living epitaph. Turning a willing cheek from Light toward darkness, this friend declares herself the fool with a megaphone on social media.

"Grief shared is grief diminished," says Elizabeth. "I thought I would get this news out of the way first so we can move on to something more cheerful."

Elizabeth tells me the phrase was a familiar saying her father used as a funeral director.

It wasn't until hours later, while having coffee at a crowded Starbucks with another girlfriend in the neighborhood, that those words about grief became a signpost with God's fingerprints all over it.

Meekly interrupting a conversation with my friend Louise, a woman gently places flyers in front of each of us on the table holding our coffees. Her hair disheveled, mascara bleeding, I notice the woman is wearing a nurse's smock underneath a violet hoodie with the nametag *Manager*.

She asks if we would be willing to sign the petition. "My daughter was killed as a pedestrian, hit by a car last month, and I'm trying to do something to change the intersection," she says quietly, wiping tears from her cheeks.

I look at the black-and-white photograph of her beautiful twenty-something daughter above words on the flyer. I clamp my hand on her thin arm and ask if she can sit down for a minute. She pulls up a chair, the box of flyers on her lap, and begins rolling her fingers around the necklace she is wearing. She tells us she is working, mostly running the vacuum and washing dishes at a doctor's office.

Death is fresh in her dark, hollow eyes, pleading for answers. This kind of thing is a mother's worst nightmare.

I tell her about how I came within an inch of losing my daughter to an eighteen-wheeler, and ask about her faith. "Do you know Jesus?" She nods but admits she can't pray yet. She reads Scripture daily for comfort. And that's when the words Elizabeth spoke drift back: *Grief shared is grief diminished.*

Repeating our stories of horror are sometimes the only comfort we can offer. *Our Father, who art in heaven, hallowed be thy name . . .* is the emergency prayer remembered in times of trauma.

Life is big like God's kingdom. Relationship is small town with Jesus. He knows your name and what you will say before you utter it. His couch is always available and bread never runs out, no matter the circumstance. A forced Sabbath can be an unexpected grace—a small portal of escape when life feels big, overwhelming, and interrupted.

Cheryl writes me with that sentiment. The mother of two sons growing into manhood, she and her husband struggle with building a real estate business during an economic downturn in the Phoenix market. And the financial stress compromises her health. She begins her letter by admitting participation in the Sabbath Society is about supporting *me*. And then the miraculous happens.

A person of influence walks up to her during a prayer meeting, telling her exactly what is wrong with her body; things she already knows, but some she isn't aware of yet. The prophetic encounter begins a fresh focus on maximizing optimal health. Her first plan of action? Making an appointment with a naturopath.

Cheryl writes,

The initial test results came back in black and white, clearly stating that my body is exhausted. In fact, Level 3 exhaustion, which is the highest level on the test. That caused me to start actually observing Sabbath. I began with part of the day and worked my way toward the whole day.

I just got the results back from the second test and it shows that things are turning around in my body in a pretty significant fashion. Even though I still am not where I need to be, the underlying causes are righting themselves. My doctor was so pleased. I think resting one day a week is a big part of the turnaround in my health.

One of the key changes Cheryl made was to stop all the *shoulds* in her daily life. Now she doesn't study the Bible and pray because she *should* but because she delights in the discipline. And changing the way she gives and receives is a new discovery for her since instituting regular times of rest. Cheryl believes that being a generous receiver is just as important as being a generous giver, admitting this is hard for her because she often places her needs at the end of a long list.

"For me, observing Sabbath is permission to take the rest I desperately need; to get over the guilt that somehow I should just be supernaturally okay. Now I want to go to the next level, so to speak, with Sabbath. The Sabbath Society has turned out to be a catalyst for huge change in my life, one tiny change at a time."

A few months later Cheryl follows up, and what I read makes me laugh and tear up:

I look back on starting Sabbath-keeping; you know, to support you. I started with Sunday afternoon, which seemed so monumental to allow myself half of a day. It seems so funny now. What was I thinking? I don't know. But at least I make myself laugh.

I had an appointment with my naturopath last week. She said she can see improvement in my health. I definitely think incorporating Sabbath has played a big part in the positive changes.

When we give sacrificially, whether 10 percent of our income, a few hours of contemplation, or one day away from work for Sabbath, we are acknowledging that God is the source of all we possess. In essence, we are saying, "I trust you to take care of me." "Steep your life in God-reality, God-initiative, God-provisions. Don't worry about missing out. You'll find all your everyday human concerns will be met" (Matthew 6:33 MSG).

Sabbath-keeping isn't a magic formula we follow in order to attain preferred outcomes, but a recognition of God's sovereignty over the minutes. When we forget God is in control of what he creates, a forced Sabbath is a reorientation so we'll remember. We're not taking a day off work for the reward of greater productivity, but a day to remember why we work. Every awakening with breath is a gift. I learned that through my daughter and those with whom I lead in the Sabbath Society.

May God's voice be an interruption of certainty—a disorientation as clear as the lines on your face.

CHAPTER SEVEN

Watch for the Arrows

Apart from The Holy we think we can improve our lives simply by progressing, getting a little more of this and then of that. But like a badly aimed arrow, the farther we go, the greater the miss.

Eugene Peterson, *The Jesus Way*

Another freak snowstorm in our coastal community interrupts school, work, and our security when a tree limb becomes a weapon, cutting through the roof. H and I have plans to fly to Dallas at the request of his boss, but all flights in Myrtle Beach are canceled due to dangerous conditions. Redemption arrives when I discover our travel plans are moved to the same weekend my agent, Chip MacGregor, is in Dallas for a writing conference. A month earlier, I signed a contract for his representation of my work, but I haven't met him in person yet. I register to attend the conference.

After a whirlwind weekend of activity with authors and ministry leaders, on Sunday, H and I sit in the Dallas airport at Love Field, staring silently at strangers pulling carry-on luggage past us. Leaning against the wall, coats draped over laps, we wait at the gate for an early morning departure, trapped in a torrent of thoughts. While children are flitting through rows of seats, marveling over giant airplanes pulled like toys on wheels across the tarmac, we're making mental assessments, replaying the past forty-eight hours.

"What have we just done?" I mumble monotone with a deadlock focus on a piece of bubble gum stuck to a pillar.

We spent Valentine's Day away from home, but our time in Dallas wasn't a romantic getaway. H's boss assumed we were coming to scout neighborhoods and schools for relocation. But instead, we surprise him with some news after lunch.

After more than a decade of dedication to a church planting movement—nearly two hundred new congregations in North America—and a time of lengthy discernment, we decide it's time to leave H's current position. And move to England. London, specifically.

Truthfully, that was the extent of our leading. We had no idea what that meant. For the first time in twenty-four years of marriage and ministry together, we sensed God asking us to take a leap of faith without knowing a hint of detail regarding outcomes. But that vision of the stop sign and moving truck in London came back to the forefront of my thoughts during times of quiet listening.

H shakes off the malaise from our time in Dallas like a dog onshore after a long swim in a giant lake. He leans over, looks at me, and says, "You aren't getting a Sabbath this week."

"No, I'm not," I agree. "To be honest, I actually forgot what day of the week it is."

Once on the plane, I find my seat, push the seat belt into the lock, and pull the strap around my waist. I close my eyes and start a mental conversation with Jesus. It begins something like this: *Your reputation is on the line now; we can't go back to the life as we've known it for more than a decade.* "I'm afraid" is basically what I'm communicating. "Remember your word to your servant, for you have given me hope. My comfort in my suffering is this:

Your promise preserves my life" (Psalm 119:49–50). As we begin the ascent, the noise of the engine overrides my inner dialogue, and movement upward somehow brings relief. Moments later, my eyes open to sun glinting outside the oval window, reflecting off the wing. The landscape below slowly drifts into Monopoly houses behind a vast array of gauzy white curtains spread over big blue Texas sky. And before I open the book in my lap, God whispers something I hold on to like a winning lottery ticket. And Samuel's words echo back to him: *Speak, for your servant is listening* (1 Samuel 3:10).

I hear an affirmation about our individual steps of faith—H's decision to quit his job before knowing the next steps and my new path toward becoming an author. Our brave yeses pull God's finger on a divine trigger, unleashing a new season of life together. As clouds transform into rows of giant cotton pulled fresh off the plant, I see an arrow in my mind's eye and hear this: *You are an arrow released from the bow, soaring into the celestial, the sacred, and into a holy moment.* "My heart has heard you say, 'Come and talk with me.' And my heart responds, 'Lord, I am coming'" (Psalm 27:8 NLT).

As I watch the lone arrow soar, arcing over the clouds, gaining momentum, he assures me that he is at work, orchestrating the pieces of our next chapter, but we won't always be able to see tangible evidence. He usually leaves bread crumbs, hints for discernment confirming we are moving in the right direction. But this time he is warning me it will be different, in the same way I can't actually see a physical arrow out my window, yet I know he is revealing a glimpse of his power and majesty. The recollection of a memorized verse of Scripture brings affirmation in the moment: "Now faith is the assurance of things hoped for, the conviction of things not seen" (Hebrews 11:1 ESV). As I watch the arrow descend into the clouds and out of my peripheral vision, I sense God warning me that once the clouds part, a whirlwind will carry us back swiftly, and the landscape will look different than we think once we land in England. Better than we imagine.

This seems weird, I think to myself. I don't mention the arrow to H right away because I worry weariness is making me delusional. Or fear is causing me to create a preferred prayerful conversation. H and I are usually on the same page as far as the things we think about, but I'm actually afraid if I mention this to him, he won't understand it. After peanuts and pretzels and a few swigs of Diet Pepsi, I divulge my (crazy) arrow story and watch his countenance perk up from his tiredness. I tell him I think our move to London and the book I'm writing are somehow linked, then lean into his shoulder and fall asleep until we see a wide expanse of the Atlantic out the window.

A few days later, Chip sends me a follow-up email with an attachment included for new authors. When I open the document, I can hardly contain a swell of emotions. The attachment is entitled *The Arrow.*

Chip sends me a resource as a normal practice of representation, a document that helps to shape a person's calling as an author. But for me, it's more than a resource. It's a confirmation of what I envisioned on the plane that day. God is gracious when we doubt him. "For I know the plans I have for you, declares the Lord, plans for welfare and not for evil, to give you a future and a hope" (Jeremiah 29:11 ESV).

He knew about the snowstorm, the change of plans that resulted in a divine appointment. He knew I would be getting a Sabbath, but not in the way I expected—on an airplane, during an intimate conversation about an arrow, eating snacks from a foil bag.

"So God blessed the seventh day and made it holy, because on it God rested from all his work that he had done in creation" (Genesis 2:3 ESV). The seventh day remains holy regardless of where we find ourselves, regardless of feelings about time and space. Sabbath remains holy and set apart because he *is* holy, different, other than. How did I miss this for decades?

I think about Noah. Noah is the stuff of storybooks, of arks, animals, rainbows, and promises, of a dove holding a twig in his beak. But Noah, it says in Genesis, was a righteous man, the only blameless person living on earth at the time. He walked in close fellowship with God (Genesis 6:9). In Hebrew, *Noah* means rest, comfort, repose.

The *only* blameless person on the earth was also the man whose name is identified with rest. Do you grasp the significance? On the sixth day, the day before God rested from all that he created, God saw all that he had made, and it was very good (1:31). Yet only one was blameless. "God created mankind in his own image, in the image of God he created them" (1:27). Noah was the spitting image of his Father, and yet he was the only kid who desired relationship. The only one of his children who went out of his way to know his Father and show love for him. The only son to ask for advice and then do what he was told. In our numbers-driven culture, measuring success as calculable and quantifiable, one success story from all the people God created would be translated as a failure with a capital *F*.

But God didn't see himself as a loser; he didn't measure the worth of his work by one blameless person on the earth. He acts out of who he is, not by how he feels. His value isn't determined by numbers of people who choose relationship with him. Oh, don't get me wrong, he had regrets (Genesis 6:6), and was deeply troubled by what he witnessed, as any father struggles with the realities associated with wayward children. But he had the one incomprehensible component that isn't dependent on circumstances: hope. God chose Noah as a remnant because hope does not disappoint; it pulls us into the future. Hope and rest are connected.

Noah saw the arrow pointing toward the future and accomplished all that God asked of him. Regardless of how foolish his actions seemed to the watching world, Noah built an ark. When we build a rhythm of rest, it is a sign of hope for a weary world.

You and I can be the remnant God uses like Noah, blameless people God looks upon with favor because we listen and trust him. Close fellowship despite living in a busy world tainted by darkness results in a Sabbath heart. God is asking us to build an ark, a safe harbor of rest constructed with hope, a bold proclamation, saving those who are perishing in their own strength.

As a result of Noah's obedience, God established a covenant with him and all of his descendants. He promised never again to destroy the earth by water and then gave Noah a sign to back it up. God gave Noah a rainbow: a bold sweep of colors as a sign that his promises are true—not just for Noah, but for future generations as well.

> Never again will the waters become a flood to destroy all life. Whenever the rainbow appears in the clouds, I will see it and remember the everlasting covenant between God and all living creatures of every kind on the earth. . . . This is the sign of the covenant I have established between me and all life on the earth.
>
> Genesis 9:15–17

The rainbow is like the wedding ring I wear on my left hand. Every time I look at it, I remember the covenant of marriage I made with my H before God.

One of God's attributes is giving us signs that his precepts are trustworthy. He instructed Moses, "This bread is to be set out before the Lord regularly, Sabbath after Sabbath, on behalf of the Israelites, as a lasting covenant" (Leviticus 24:8). Then the Lord said to Moses: "The Israelites are to observe the Sabbath, celebrating it for the generations to come as a lasting covenant" (Exodus 31:16). In the book of Ezekiel, he spells it out clearly: "I gave them . . . my 'Sabbaths,' a kind of signpost erected between me and them to show them that I, God, am in the business of making them holy" (Ezekiel 20:11–12 MSG).

God gave Noah a rainbow, Moses some bread, and he gave me an arrow. What is the sign he is giving you? If you are looking up at the ceiling and pondering what your sign might be, stop right there for a minute and let me tell you what it is. God gives *all of us* Sabbath as a sign of covenant between us, a reminder that He is Lord of who we are and all that we possess. Sabbath is love written large, declaring God is good; he remembers the promises between us.

I want to be like Noah. One walking against popular norms in our culture for the sake of intimate union, trusting a rainbow will appear on the horizon. I want to be an arrow pointing people toward Hope, a landscape that looks different and better than we can imagine.

I drive four hours each way to visit my friend Margaret for the day. When I learn she is in South Carolina, speaking at a conference, we decide to rendezvous because four hours away is geographically closer than her home in Denver. This may be my only chance to see her before we move to England, so I cancel everything I have on the calendar.

Let me know when you arrive. I receive a text on my phone from Margaret while I'm in transit. In the hotel lobby, our eyes meet across an empty expanse of floor and ceiling. We embrace for an extended period like an exclamation point capping off months of email exchanges. Being physically present is good medicine for both of us.

She's already been out, scouting out restaurants for us. "I need to take my coat upstairs," she tells me, "it's warming up outside."

For several blocks, we walk through downtown Greenville, past rows of windows full of souvenirs, T-shirts, sweet treats, and household goods. We stroll behind people walking dogs and pushing strollers, past couples sipping coffee around café tables. Sunshine beckons; the end of winter is nearing. Standing in line inside a small restaurant, the spicy smell of taco meat makes my mouth water. *How did Margaret know I love Mexican food?*

We talk about writing and publishing, when I notice she's carrying her dog, Hershey, in a purse hanging over her shoulder. I'm overcome with Margaret's generosity, sacrificing time for me during a busy season of speaking engagements. After returning our trays and dishes to where we got them, we continue our slow meander back to the hotel, through a garden path beside a small waterfall. And though there isn't anything earth-shattering spoken between us, I sense our four-hour conversation is a sacred window of time God has opened for us.

Nearing the city center, I notice a woman wearing a foam arrow on her head, like the ones Steve Martin made famous in his comedy routines. I wouldn't have given that arrow a second glance, except for the way God had been using arrows to garner my attention. It's as if my walk with Margaret is a sign of his faithful promises and presence with us, the same way he used a rainbow with Noah. With the hotel in plain sight, we begin wrapping up our conversation, when Leif, Margaret's husband, appears out of nowhere, standing in a shady alcove. He's waiting to talk through some surface details regarding Margaret's speaking engagement and making sure she isn't overdoing it.

Pulling Hershey from the carrier, Margaret hands the miniature black bundle to Leif, and the dog rests its head on Leif's chest, a mere dot on his towering six-foot-eight frame. They have more questions for me about London—moving, transitioning, timetables—all for which I have vague answers, when suddenly, a small crowd of people with ice cream cones stop and begin engaging with Leif. I assume they want to pet the dog, but the longer I listen I realize they know Margaret personally. They are in the area to attend the conference.

We exchange greetings and I'm pulled into the embrace of one of the women. It's as if I'm looking into the face of Jesus. She pulls back and smiles in welcome. Around her neck is an arrow anchored by a chain on the point and fletching. I start to ask her where she purchased the necklace, and then realize I'm missing the point. God is near, assuring me he hasn't forgotten his covenant even when I doubt his faithfulness and timing.

Isn't this what friends do? They show up and surprise you when you least expect it. Creating rhythms of whitespace in your schedule lets you know the details matter. Friends remind us we are loved when we are afraid of the future.

As I become aware of the arrows showing up in unlikely places, I begin to document details like a detective searching for the source of mysterious love notes. I encourage the Sabbath Society to join me in identifying details they notice as they incorporate Sabbath as a weekly rhythm. Alee responds first:

Worthiness, Shelly, is what God has been teaching me through Sabbath. He has been revealing to me his thoughts concerning us, his children. Besides being a mother and wife, I am a full-time college student in my last semester of classes before preparing for clinicals. My workload is overwhelming and endless. I spent over forty-eight hours in class and studying last week alone, and there was still much more on my to-do list as far as my studies are concerned. My list for this week looks very similar. It is Friday afternoon. I have a project and an online test due by Monday evening. Joy.

Alee communicates that she is thankful for the opportunity to attend classes, but is overwhelmed by the challenges being a student presents. Sabbath has looked far different for her family than it has in the past. Most of us have our own set Sabbath days, but for some those days revolve from one week to another.

One of the things I have learned during the past ten or eleven weeks is that I matter, tremendously. I am worth setting aside everything else for the insane workload, the demands of family members with to-do lists needing my attention, housework, cooking—everything that was not accomplished during the week. Sabbath was doable when I had the time to plan for it, to ready myself and my household. But Sabbath comes, ready or not. It arrives like an old friend quietly knocking on the door, asking if you'd like to come out and play for the day, and my childlike response each week has been a resounding yes! I not only need the break and the rest, but my soul demands it. I am worth my time. My relationships with God and others are far better off if I am committed to meeting my own needs. Sabbath allows for

*this. The God and Creator of the universe deems me worthy
of rest, and I relish in it.*

Alee's current life stage illustrates something important for all
of us. Choosing a day outside of Sunday to Sabbath isn't second
best among the alternatives. We are worthy of time set apart for
rest because God is worthy of our attention. When life is buzzing
all around us, making a day restful lies in the details.

Reserve a favorite tea or coffee for Sabbath mornings and look
forward to sipping a different brew once a week. Indulge in a
hearty breakfast if you don't normally allow yourself that. Spend
extra time lingering in your pajamas and read another chapter
in a favorite book before showering. Pray and listen intently
instead of leaving the TV on as background noise. Leave the
dishes on the counter and explore a new part of the city. Enjoy
a fresh face (without makeup). Not looking in the mirror for a
day can be a kind of restful grace. Intentionally connect with
people, not because you need something from them but because
you want to cultivate their friendship. Laugh until your stomach
hurts. Give yourself permission to "waste time" for the sake of
rest. All the small choices in the details are arrows pointing to
a day set apart, communion with the One who created the day
in the first place.

Sabbath rhythms become sentinels to those around you. My
family has learned to expect a bevy of savory and sweet smells
wafting from the kitchen in preparation for Sabbath. When we
sit down to dinner at sundown and I light the Shabbat candles, it
is a sign that rest is what is most important on the agenda for the
next twenty-four hours.

Joy is a Brit who lives an ongoing battle with the symptoms of
Myalgic Encephalopathy (ME), a severe and debilitating fatigue
resulting in painful muscles and joints, disordered sleep, gastric
disturbances, poor memory and concentration.[1] Learning how to
practice self-compassion as someone who lives with weakness and

weariness as a default position, she admits running on empty most of the time and vacillating to full steam ahead whenever a burst of energy makes a sudden appearance. In the past, the extra exertion experienced during those bursts often results in chastisement for falling into the busy trap.

In the same way Alee's busy season of life creates a dilemma about when she and those in her household Sabbath, Joy finds difficulty in attempting Sabbath on a set timetable because of her unpredictable health issues. She writes,

> *It's very hard to rest and unwind at a particular time, especially if that's when I have some inspiration to write or more get-up-and-go than usual. Essentially, I'm far more compassionate and understanding toward others than I ever succeed at being toward myself. I'm thinking about a time of resting differently now and realize it's actually okay to indulge myself a little—sit in my comfiest chair, read a fascinating book just because, and relax in being a person of worth in God's eyes, whether I am at all active or not.*

Body, mind, and soul more easily enter true rest when we understand and then accept our worthiness based on who we are, not on what we do.

> For you formed my inward parts; you knitted me together in my mother's womb. I praise you, for I am fearfully and wonderfully made. Wonderful are your works; my soul knows it very well. My frame was not hidden from you, when I was being made in secret, intricately woven in the depths of the earth. Your eyes saw my unformed substance; in your book were written, every one of them, the days that were formed for me, when as yet there was none of them.
>
> Psalm 139:13–16 ESV

We can be known and yet completely unknowable at the same time. We can learn a lot about someone—their triumphs, successes, and failures—by scrolling through feeds on Facebook, listening to clips on YouTube, and flipping through photos on Instagram. We can know a lot about someone without actually meeting them in person in the same way we can learn about God through reading Scripture, inspirational books, and listening to sermons. But how much of our faith journey is firsthand experience and not just what we know *about* him? Information helps us to know about God, but Sabbath allows us to encounter him. When our life falls apart without warning, it isn't the data that we rely on but the relationship we've cultivated through meaningful, ongoing conversation.

Abigail is a twenty-something from New Zealand who wrote to me in response to one of the Sabbath Society letters, an admission about what she's been relying on. She describes herself as someone who looks successful on the outside with gifts and service, useful to others in a myriad of ways. But being needed subtly became Abigail's identity:

What should I be doing? And what am I doing wrong? Two questions always on my mind, and having to choose between options was enough to make me cry. I thought if I wasn't obedient, God's plans would fall apart. He needed me to serve! To build his kingdom! And if I failed and he didn't love me anymore, then I truly did have nothing.

Exercise became Abigail's choice for numbing the pain of uncertainty. The endorphins took her mind to a peaceful place, but all that changed one day when she got hypothermia while trying to swim across a mountain lake. Alone and out of cell phone range, she began falling asleep on the side of the lake as a result of exhaustion. Suddenly, a still, small voice awakened her, *"Get to the car, put the heater on, and don't stop moving."* And just like Noah, she listened, obeyed, and managed to get out of the mountain pass and back to safety:

I'm finally learning that true rest is only accessible through faith in Christ. Not exercise, worship, Bible reading, meditation, service, or loving others. There is no rest in being useless when you already feel worthless. It feels much safer to lean on self-righteousness than dare to humble myself and believe again. This is not about doing rest; this is about being loved for doing nothing! Saying no to obligation and yes to Sabbath is my favorite thing.

Eugene Peterson says,

Faith has to do with marrying Invisible and Visible. When we engage in an act of faith we give up control, we give up sensory confirmation of reality; we give up insisting on head-knowledge as our primary means of orientation of life.[2]

In an evolution of intimacy in our friendship with Jesus, we begin looking for letters about winning the lottery to slide into the mailbox and sometimes we become disappointed when what we find are pieces of junk mail, impersonal words with the goal of obtaining something from us. But God is sending love letters by way of divine arrows, pointing to what may seem like random details but are significant signposts of his covenant with us.

We incarnate what is hidden in plain sight by watching and listening attentively to the world around us. On the day we choose to abide on Sabbath, he appears like a gift delivered on our doorstep or an arrow shooting across a cloudless sky. He longs for relationship more than anything we can do for him. The signs are all around us. Watch for the arrows.

CHAPTER EIGHT

Extravagant
Wastefulness

Play and Sabbath are joined at the hip, and sometimes we rest
best when we play hardest.

Mark Buchanan, *The Rest of God*

From a park bench, beneath a canopy of ancient trees with long
tendrils swaying from Spanish moss, I hear the distant sound of
an ambulance siren and birds chirping in their various "dialects."
A middle-aged couple walk by, heads down, as if I am invisible.

Yellow leaves pirouette six feet above my head onto the pages
of my journal. *Tick . . . tick . . . tick . . . tic-tic-tic . . . tic-tic-tic . . .*
raindrops begin to fall, and before I can put my pen and journal
inside my bag, the rain ceases.

Our membership at this favorite haunt in the area, Brookgreen
Gardens, has lapsed, but I decide to pay full price for entrance on a
quiet Sunday. While the kids rest on the couch watching a favorite
television series and H meets with people of influence across the

Atlantic in London, I grab my camera bag and journal for some time of reflection. The whitespace of Sabbath is a safe harbor when emotions trick me into believing that reasoning is a solution for anxiety. Trusting in God's providence seems foolish as the days drag on. We've made the decision to leave a job, a paycheck, and security without knowing the details of where we are going next. H is scouting the landscape, investigating potential options, and sharing our Macedonian call to London with bishops, priests, friends, and cohorts. The unknowns, when I spend time looping through each of them in detail, tend to make me a ball of anxiousness tangled up with self-doubt.

Brookgreen Gardens is a place I anticipate returning to in memory with deep fondness for what its quiet beauty represents. It is where I learned to listen with acute attention to the cadence of God's voice, the wilderness of isolation that creates a clear path for writing through the heaviness I carry. Though my heart has already left for England, years in this coastal community are a beacon of intimacy in our friendship, where I have cultivated a craving for the nearness of Jesus in my inmost being.

Pulling out a cardigan, I wrap it around my shoulders when a cool breeze chills and blows hair into my face. The sun slowly shifts, creating shadows, a signpost in nature that pulls my mind back to obligation. I begin mentally scouring my refrigerator and pantry for what I can reheat on paper plates for dinner tonight. It is seventy degrees outside, but snow is predicted in the Carolinas this week.

With H worlds away in England, I'm anxious. We are desperate for the arrival of spring after a hard spiritual winter. The garage floor is carpeted with boxes holding picture frames, dishes, and a bevy of items ready for consignment. Though the timeline for our departure to England is a mystery, this meander through Brookgreen is a sacred pause, a bon voyage I sense with unexplainable confidence in my spirit. Journaling the details, I toast God with my pen, celebrating what he has done in and through us while here.

For some, brackets of time alone on a park bench to journal the sights, sounds, and smells of a wide expanse in nature is an illustration of extravagant wastefulness. Or a lavish indulgence allotted those who are retired from work life. *What is this accomplishing? How is this helping me get to London? Overcome anxious feelings?*

"Idleness is not just a vacation, an indulgence or a vice," writer Tim Kreider observes.

> It is as indispensable to the brain as vitamin D is to the body, and deprived of it we suffer a mental affliction as disfiguring as rickets. The space and quiet that idleness provides is a necessary condition for standing back from life and seeing it whole, for making unexpected connections and waiting for the wild summer lightning strikes of inspiration—it is, paradoxically, necessary to getting any work done.[1]

Research reveals that when we relax, or enter into a window of daydreaming, the brain does not slow down or stop working at all, but rather many important mental processes happen during those times in the same physiological way the brain works when we sleep at night. Accruing evidence suggests that these times of rest are important for recalling personal memories, imagining the future, and feeling social emotions with moral connotations.[2]

In Sabbath, we allow our brain to make sense of our busy lives. We process what we have learned during the other six days of the week and apply meaning to what we've overlooked while moving at a frenetic pace. Sitting on a park bench, I stare into space, replay conversations, wrestle through unresolved questions like a mathematician solving an equation. I reflect on previous decisions, and during introspection, mull over the events of the past few months. I rewrite negative inner dialogue into a positive, hopeful outlook. Epiphanies come in the shower, alone on a quiet walk, staring out the window of my office, driving in a silent car, and while listening to the sound of bird chatter in Brookgreen Gardens.

What do we need to get done this weekend? It's often the first question H asks me on Saturday mornings, after we've slept in, slumped around in our pajamas, and passed the morning hours reading, playing video games (for him), and sipping our coffee and tea (for me), taking the liberty of slowing more than usual when we aren't shackled by obligations.

And can I be honest? Some days I don't want to be productive. I don't care about getting things done. But this convincing voice inside my head tells me otherwise. I'll feel somehow less than, lazy, irresponsible if I'm not doing or accomplishing something from the long list. I trick myself into believing I'll find a deep sense of fulfillment if my garden is perfectly manicured or my kitchen painted a different color, a sense of ultimate satisfaction in writing an article for a magazine rather than absorbing what the quiet wants to say to me. I assume *busy* is a badge of belonging associated with value. Instead, the result is exhaustion with all that idealism sucked right out of me. H asks me the question about what needs doing not because he needs an activity to keep him busy, but because he longs to have his finger on the pulse of the family heartbeat.

In a culture where it is common to attach value with utility, we train ourselves to feel good about our ministries, our church activities, sports teams, livelihoods, and parenting, as long as what we do provides a measure of usefulness and positive calculable outcomes.

Mika Häkkinen is a two-time Formula One champion, but it took him seven years on the circuit to win his first Grand Prix. He credits his legacy of success to mentor Dr. Aki Hintsa, who "helped him sharpen his focus on the track by helping him to allay concerns he had off the track."[3]

Dr. Hintsa is a specialist in orthopedic and trauma surgery and the founder of Hintsa Performance. While working in Africa as a missionary doctor, he observed the training routines of the elite Ethiopian distance runners and came to the conclusion that success is derived from holistic well-being. The fast-paced environment of racing provided the ideal context for Hintsa to put his ideas to the ultimate test.[4]

Most athletes want to know what they can *do* to be better than their rivals. How can they really get the most out of a single day? Hinsta's answer is simple: Get a good night's sleep. "Operating three nights in a row on just five hours' sleep is equivalent to driving a car drunk," says Hinsta. "Mika agrees; you need to rest more than you train, he says, because you just can't improve while you're tired."[5] Not a formula for success you would expect to hear from a top Formula One athlete.

When value is tied only to tangible results, the sacrament of presence becomes a dying significance. As we lead mission trips to Africa and meet hospitable Rwandans, we discover how our pragmatic approach to ministry becomes corrosive. What we should consider a heart investment of time becomes a waste of time. My Rwandan friends use a common saying when we arrive on their red turf: "Rwandans have time and Americans have clocks." This couldn't be a more convicting yet accurate statement. Take twelve Americans on the trip of their lifetime, and the first question they ask? "What are we going to be *doing* today?" In order for a mission trip to be worth the investment of time and resources, mission boards, financial supporters, and missionaries on the ground want to see measurable outcomes. But what if God's highest expectation in the journey to a needy culture is engaging the sacrament of presence, being with people because we love them? Is our time with people valuable even if the time can't be calculated into measured outcomes? According to my friend Archbishop Emmanuel Kolini, our undivided attention is the most precious resource we can give people in his country.

People in third-world countries teach those of us in the West that our poverty isn't in tangible assets but in our inability to practice pausing. We know we need Sabbath, but we don't know how to make Sabbath a reality. "Wasting time" in order to be present isn't justifiable, so we struggle with how to find usefulness.

Selah. It's a curious word mentioned seventy-four times in the Bible. Scholars aren't unified about the definition, but most agree that *Selah* means "pause and think about that."

In May, H and I travel back to London to celebrate our wedding anniversary, paired with another spiritual scouting trip and Alpha Leadership Conference. We are perched high in a loggia box of the Royal Albert Hall, surrounded by six thousand people from around the world, when Father Raniero Cantalamessa, preacher to the Papal Household, is invited to pray and release attendees for lunch. Everyone present stands to their feet as Cantalamessa bows his head. And we wait in that posture of submission, in silence, for three minutes.

What is he doing? We wonder. *Is he okay? Why isn't he saying anything?* The longer the silence lingers, the more people begin fidgeting, looking at cell phones, lifting their heads, and glancing sideways at each other.

Afterward, it's clear to me that Father Raniero was practicing Selah, something I assume he does often as a Catholic priest. In some translations of the Bible, *Selah* is defined as "stop and listen" or "to measure or weigh what is being said." Father Raniero was weighing the meaning of what was being asked of him in that moment. He was practicing the pause and listening for God's voice before doing something that is most likely second nature for him.

Mark Twain said, "The right word may be effective, but no word was ever as effective as a rightly timed pause."[6] I think of how many times I've been asked to do something I'm good at and breezed right through without stopping to listen first. Or felt the weight of silence in a conversation and filled the awkwardness with chatter. Three minutes of silence became the most profound statement of the conference for me. The long pause before reciting a prayer reminded us that we wait on God, not so we can speak *for* him but so he can speak *through* us. Father Raniero illustrated that pausing might be the most brave thing people witness in us. And he gave fresh meaning to this directive in the Scriptures: "Be still, and know that I am God" (Psalm 46:10).

Silence outside of sacred space can be just as disarming. Actor Bryan Cranston, best known for his portrayal of Walter White on the hit television series *Breaking Bad*, adopted what he refers to as silent Mondays.[7] After he left the show that made him wildly famous, he began playing larger-than-life President Lyndon B. Johnson on stage eight times a week in the play *All the Way*. Concerned about the long-term strength of his vocal cords, he took a cue from fellow actress Audra McDonald, who was following the advice of an ear, nose, and throat doctor, shutting down her voice one day a week to keep it healthy. She incorporated Mondays as her silent day, and Cranston decided to follow her lead as a preventive measure.

On Mondays, Cranston runs errands, eats in restaurants, and lives life as usual, except instead of using his voice, he carries a little notepad or uses a white board to communicate. He writes down things like "What is the soup of the day?" And when people give him curious looks, he shows them a static message that reads, "Doctors orders: Vocal rest, not talking." And perhaps more curious than the odd stares Cranston receives on Monday is the way people respond back to his notes.

They whisper.

Why do you think people whisper when they learn Cranston can't talk? Silence changes the profane to sacred. Silence is equated with reverence and awe, something otherworldly and beyond our control. Silence disrobes busyness and makes it holy. Walk into an empty church, a funeral home, or the hospital room of a sick person. Sabbath is silence—a faint whisper breaking into a loud and busy world.

In Finland, silence is a marketable resource. Known as a rather quiet country, the Country Brand Delegation had been looking for a marketable theme since 2008. And while professionals were looking for a way to garner some noise about their country, ironically, they discovered that silence sells. A marketing campaign was born with slogans exclaiming, "Silence, Please," "No talking, but action," and "Handmade in Finnish silence," all creatively provoking an influx of new tourism.[8]

In a busy world that prescribes more—more exercise, more diets, more involvement in community, more engagement on social media, more ways to make money, more education, and more resources for ramping up productivity—a rhythm of daily silence and weekly Sabbath is making a (quiet) comeback.

Solitude is a state of being, an isolation or aloneness that God uses in our lives for specific reasons. And solitude of the heart is an attitude of quietness; a state of living unguarded, confident, and stable despite circumstance.[9] Solitude of the heart can maintain a standard of steadiness whether living in the midst of urban sprawl or hidden down a country lane. A state of inner solitude doesn't depend on the outside world, the reception of others, or circumstance, and it is most often contagious to those who find anxiety and emotional upheaval the norm of life. The more we experience the work of solitude within us, we begin to identify the rested from the restless, the discontented from the contented, the broken from the whole; we begin to decipher failure, missteps, and successes through a heart aching for eternity.

Author Brennan Manning said he spent an hour each morning in silent prayer. He wrote,

> Deciding what I most need out of life, carefully calculating my next move, and generally allowing my autonomous self to run amuck inflates my sense of self-importance and reduces the God of my incredible journey to the role of spectator on the sidelines. It is only the wisdom and perspective gleaned from an hour of silent prayer each morning that prevents me from running for CEO of the universe.[10]

Have you trained yourself to pause? Do you pay attention to your heart, warning you it's time to slow down? Or do you need someone to tell you to stop because you're too busy to notice the warning signals? Pause and think about what God is saying to you, so you don't find yourself in the path of danger or lost without purpose. Rhythmic pauses help us remember where we are going when life becomes crowded and disorienting.

Nearly every time *Selah* is mentioned in the Psalms, there is a definitive topic addressed and a heart change afterward: renewed direction, increased faith, deeper appreciation for God's direction. Who knew daydreaming out your office window could be so revolutionary to your work?

"May God be gracious to us and bless us and make his face shine on us. Selah" (Psalm 67:1). This passage in Psalm 67 is a common liturgy used for Sunday worship in the church I attend, but what does "his face shine on us" really mean? *Selah* is a clue that I need to stop and think about it. Have you ever had someone you haven't thought about in years come to mind and then bumped into them somewhere random? Or needed a car repair that would break your budget and then received an unexpected refund check? Lost your way and a kind stranger showed up out of nowhere with directions? These are all ways in which God's face shines on us. And a heart change often results.

Some people might call these chance encounters coincidences, but for those of us who know friendship with Jesus, Paul's words echo from 2 Corinthians. It started when God said, "'Light up the darkness!' and our lives filled up with light as we saw and understood God in the face of Christ, all bright and beautiful. If you only look at *us*, you may well miss the brightness" (4:5–7 MSG).

Rather than allow uncertainty about our future to snuff out the brightness of God's face shining upon us, I practice Selah during our May adventure in London. H and I are filled with expectancy as we walk along crowded city streets, past red phone booths, double-decker buses, and black taxi cabs. English culture speaks our language, but an overload of stimulating activity threatens to deplete joy as our oxygen. When H asks me what I want to do with some free hours on Sabbath, my response is to sit somewhere inspiring and write in my journal. London boasts a bevy of Selah opportunities.

Sitting alone on the only empty chair left in the courtyard at the Victoria and Albert Museum, I watch four young girls sprawled out on a verdant carpet, each with a different shade of ginger hair. Their curls bounce beneath felt hats trimmed in dark satin ribbon. They are each wearing black leather jackets. One hunches over a book in her lap, her legs crossed beneath a long floral skirt as she turns the pages.

An impromptu theatrical gathering of young children splash in the nearby fountain, hiking their pants above their knees until it becomes a nuisance. One boy wades unabashedly in his underwear and a striped navy sweater.

Sun is usually in short supply in London. On this day, people are soaking it up like a sponge, abandoning whatever is on their agenda. Pigeons pad tiny red feet through a dense patch of grass in front of me, serpentining through groups of people. Unlike me, they are unaffected by the number of foreign dialects being spoken. Laughter sounds the same in any language.

In *Playdates with God*, Laura Boggess writes, "It's no accident that the word *question* contains the word *quest*. When was the last time I gave curiosity free rein? When did I last let myself get lost in wondering, let exploration lead instead of a goal? When we let go of preferred outcomes—from striving for a certain goal—our imagination is opened up and the years are peeled away, freeing us to wonder."[11]

Instead of wandering through a museum or sightseeing somewhere different, I lose myself in watching people give themselves permission to playfully rest. Perspective is lifted and joy fuels my pen. Engulfed in wonder, this kind of solitude is a prescription for healing loneliness.

Paradoxically, the solitude of Brookgreen Gardens intensified the ache of loneliness. In South Carolina, our work is finished. We have no projects to tie up, no titles granting access into new opportunities, few friends in which to find consolation. Lonely, yet aware I am not alone.

On many days, isolation led me to listen to my tears for where my heart was beating with passion, to keep vigil with prayer partners pleading heaven on my behalf, to trust in the mystery more than my situation. Reading books, watching movies, polling relatives, and scrolling social media feeds were no longer my choices for numbing the pain of uncertainty. And then one day, while drying the dishes, of all things, God stripped away my greatest illusion. My whole body was shaking on the inside, restless with insecurity.

In the past, I assumed the details of my life falling into place were a result of faith rooted in relationship with Jesus. I had dotted every *i* with the truth of Scripture and crossed every *t* with repentance. But when life's details were no longer tangible, secure, and predictable, a void in the familiar created a noticeable hole in my belief system. Subtly, I had replaced the need for Jesus with the need for certainty. The need for certainty about our future became my idol, and that revelation, my undoing.

God was testing my relationship to him. He was waiting to see if my faith was built with roots *in* him or what I knew *about* him. And I believe he waits in that same posture when we approach Sabbath. Is Sabbath something we do to build deep roots *in* him or is it what we know *about* him? Slowly, through surrender and trust, we exchange loneliness for a heart of solitude, fear as a reaction to powerlessness for love as a response of acceptance. In Sabbath, we learn how to find contentment, like a child wading through water with her pants rolled up.

Henri Nouwen instructs, "Instead of running away from our loneliness and trying to forget or deny it, we have to protect it and turn it into a fruitful solitude. To live a spiritual life we must first find the courage to enter into the desert of our loneliness and to change it by gentle and persistent efforts into a garden of solitude. The movement from loneliness to solitude, however, is the beginning of any spiritual life because it is the movement from the restless senses to the restful spirit, from the outward-reaching cravings to the inward-reaching search, from the fearful clinging to the fearless play."[12]

I can't remember the last time I played without equating the time with what I could get out of it. Or delighted in a run, bike ride, or a swim not to log miles and burn calories but because I found pleasure in the pursuit. What about social media? When was the last time you took a photo without thinking about sharing what you experienced with the masses? Or created something beautiful without needing a response from your friends on Facebook? Enjoyed a respite with your family without sharing the everyday account of how the time away was a blessing? When was the last time you engaged in something for the sheer joy of being with God?

Joy that comes from playfulness wasn't common in my household growing up. As the child of an alcoholic, the natural emotion of joy was lost in the fear of waiting for the other shoe to drop. Moments of fun almost always included cloud cover on my emotions as a way of avoiding what I assumed would be inevitable disappointment. I am in a slow recovery process with what Brené Brown coins in her book *Daring Greatly* as foreboding joy.[13] When everything is going well, my emotions tell me (wrongly) that disaster is coming, so I brace myself for the worst. Instead of taking my chances with a zip line, I imagine myself as a quadriplegic and my family shackled with caretaking. Once I opted out of a hula dancing event hosted at my best friend's fortieth birthday celebration, hiding behind my camera to capture the memory instead of participating. A physical reaction of anxiety made my chest heavy and legs wobble when I thought about making a fool of myself dancing in a hula skirt in front of girlfriends.

Foreboding joy is a fast-forward through the details, rehearsing what we assume might happen when we feel vulnerable. And usually we imagine the worst. This kind of fear is what makes play terrifying. Brown says, "When we spend our lives (knowingly or unknowingly) pushing away vulnerability, we can't hold space open for the uncertainty, risk, and emotional exposure of joy."[14]

I'm not good at spending time in unapologetic playfulness, and this is exactly why I need Sabbath. Brown's research justifies that there is a similarity between the biological need for play and our body's need for rest.[15] So I wrote to the Sabbath Society, saying,

Let's give ourselves permission this week to play for the sheer joy of it and see how it informs our rest. I'm going to pull out my watercolors and the new book I received as a gift from one of our Sabbath Society peeps, and perhaps jump

on my bike to investigate new places I haven't seen yet. Who knows, I may end up on the beach if the weather lives up to the forecast. What will you do?

Natalie writes,

Play has been a big part of my life for the past month. I spent twenty-seven out of twenty-eight nights on the road. First, I went to a nature writing class in Yellowstone with my dad. We hiked, camped, looked at the sky, and met some really wonderful people. I sang at the Mammoth Hot Springs Hotel with a Yellowstone friend. After I came home, I helped pack up the family and traveled to Rapid City, South Dakota. We spent two and a half weeks there—working, playing, hiking, touring, and home-schooling—while my husband fulfilled work responsibilities. Cell phone coverage was rare. Wi-Fi was available a mile away, but even when I had the option, my iPad would receive but not send. The to-do list was mostly powerless.

And then Natalie explains a surprising outcome after a month of play. "I am beginning to understand and embrace a long period of waiting. Words of others and God's timing came together in a way that brought clarity while we were off playing."

An allowance for unbridled joy through playdates with God on Sabbath can provide the same result as a quiet, meditative retreat. Extravagant wastefulness with time might prove the most productive thing you choose for yourself.

CHAPTER NINE

Uncertainty: Rest and Love Are Connected

> Sometimes when I think I'm waiting on God I wonder if he's actually waiting on me.
>
> Emily Freeman, *Simply Tuesday*

Baby powder? Why do I smell baby powder in my neighborhood?

On a walk, I round the corner of a street adjacent to my house, checking out each flowerpot and residence I walk past. I'm perusing gardens, porches, dense patches of forest, for something new to capture through my camera lens. Kneeling down to frame a carpet of leaves illuminated by a swath of morning light, my senses are apprehended by an unusual aroma.

Perhaps it's the smell of a dryer sheet filtering through a vent or young children playing nearby. Back on my feet on the edge of the road, I turn like the second hand on a wall clock, scrutinizing the fragrance, when the stillness apprehends me. Tweets from birds are the only sounds I'm identifying. No whir of a dryer, chatter of young voices—all is quiet, when suddenly the word *birth* comes to the forefront of my thoughts.

Get ready. God is about to birth something. Those words activate an internal adrenaline rush. The smell of baby powder is a sign—an arrow pointing to something new, fresh, celebratory—a fulfillment of a long-awaited expectation for the future. I don't know what this new season will look like, if anything about the details will resemble our past experience. All I know is that I will recognize the covenant by the unmistakable way God shows up as a sweet aroma.

Author Lauren Winner says,

> The profound work that smell does on and for us presumes absence. People separated by time and space—that baby longing for his mother, the mother pining for the children who have left her empty nest—are reconnected through smell. Smell keeps us close to one another in our absence.[1]

The longer I wait in the uncomfortable place of transition, the more I assume God is absent. But the smell of baby powder brings revelation of his inscrutable closeness. An invisible sign I translate as preparation for the next season and sign of hope.

During the gestation period of a dream—waiting for the arrival of something new he is creating within us—everything becomes an altar until the actual day of fulfillment, or a frustration. It's really a choice, isn't it?

The preferred future of our children, timing in transitions, the security of an address, health, job title, numbers in the bank account—all these details bring a sense of comfort and security with them. But when any one or all of those things become unknowns, we have a choice about letting go of the need for certainty or clinging to methods of self-protection. We face the same choices about Sabbath when uncertainty pervades the atmosphere of our week.

Lying outside on the porch with a blanket over my legs on Sabbath, I read this quote from *The Gifts of Imperfection*. It will become the theme of my next letter to the Sabbath Society.

Brené Brown writes, "Another example of how our need for certainty sabotages our intuition is when we ignore our gut's warning to slow down, gather more information, or reality check our expectations."[2]

I think her words apply to us, no matter where we find ourselves on the pilgrimage of Sabbath-keeping: just starting out or years into the journey.

The need for certainty sabotages the freedom God intended in Sabbath. We struggle with a need to know if we give up the time, our lives won't fall apart the following week. All the while, our soul screams for connection with the one who knows us best, but we ignore the still, small voice for the sake of accomplishment and productivity.

Can I tell you something? Everything in me wanted to play hooky on Sabbath last week by working on all the things left undone. I have writing deadlines in addition to everyday posts on the blog, and I'm behind on goals despite writing for hours and hours every day. The house was a mess and we had shopping plans with the kids, which meant nothing got checked off my list in preparation for a day of rest.

But I took the risk and it was worth it. I let all the most pressing items go in exchange for reading and prayer time, even a short bike ride. And by sundown on Sunday, I felt like a kid on Christmas morning—full of joy and gratitude.

Is your gut warning you to slow down and you're avoiding it because of the fear of what might happen? Can I encourage you to let go and fill up with the peace of God's goodness? He's patiently waiting for you to slow down so he can express his love for you.

You may be surprised by what you accomplish in doing a whole lot of nothing in order to listen.

Michelle writes back, "Two Sundays ago, I freaked out and worked on my book edits instead of Sabbathing. The guilt was horrendous! But I didn't think I would be able to enjoy the day with the stress hanging over my head. The good news is that the next week, I still had book edits to do, but I took a Sabbath instead, and it was so, so worth it. I think I got more done on Monday because of it. Good lesson learned."

A short time later, I face a similar dilemma. Away for a solitary writing retreat in a beach house located near the town where H and I previously pastored a church, I find myself weighing options at sundown on Saturday. Do I continue writing? Or do I take the day off? Is it a prudent, responsible use of my time to take a Sabbath from writing as usual when the reason why I've left my family for a week is to produce chapters of this book? As I ponder, I remember how God continues to redeem my time when I offer it back to him. Trust is a big part of Sabbath-keeping. *Do you trust me?* It's the question I hear him ask me every Saturday as the sun slowly descends over work left undone.

On Sunday, after church, instead of rushing back to the beach house for more writing, I enjoy a reunion with some girlfriends over tomato soup and grilled fontina, when they ask what activities are acceptable on Sabbath. I tell them whatever you do that doesn't feel like work, that's what you do on Sabbath. It's different for each of us.

For some, embarking on a creative project feels restful, and for others it feels like carrying around an eighty-pound weight. Some find napping restorative while others receive the same results by taking a hike. Gardening is good for my soul while others find weeding a burden. Once, my friend Natalie wrote to tell me about a particularly temperate Sabbath when she was living in Iowa: "When we drove into our driveway after church, our neighbor stood up from her work in her flower garden, walked over to us, and apologized for gardening on the Sabbath. I was flabbergasted that anyone would feel the need to apologize for such a thing. Although I assured her that she didn't need to apologize to me, today I would have had better words to share about freedom."

Natalie's encounter with a neighbor is reminiscent of a Sabbath stroll Jesus made with the disciples. As they ambled through a field, some began pulling off heads of grain and munching on them to quiet growling stomachs. And the Pharisees interpreted an intuitive response to hunger pains as breaking the Sabbath. *Really?* That's how Jesus responds to their accusations:

> There is far more at stake here than religion. If you had any idea what this Scripture meant—'I prefer a flexible heart to an inflexible ritual'—you wouldn't be nitpicking like this. The Son of Man is no lackey to the Sabbath; he's in charge.
>
> Matthew 12:6–8 MSG

After leaving that field of grain, he entered a meeting place where a man with a crippled hand was in need of healing. And once again, rules were dictating an inflexible mindset when the Pharisees asked Jesus, "Is it legal to heal on the Sabbath?" From a flexible heart, Jesus instructs them about the importance of context in Sabbath-keeping:

> Is there a person here who, finding one of your lambs fallen into a ravine, wouldn't, even though it was a Sabbath, pull it out? Surely kindness to people is as legal as kindness to animals!
>
> Matthew 12:11–14 MSG

Sabbatarianism is a word used to describe a movement within Protestantism. Proponents believe that to observe Sabbath properly, codes of behavior and law must be followed in order to make the practice legitimate, taking what God intended as a freedom and turning it into a spiritual hoop for justification. When the goal is controlling people and circumstances, anything can become an idol replacing God's sovereignty, even my need for certainty. Considering context in terms of how you rest keeps Sabbath rhythms flexible. Sheila writes with an example of how that looks for her:

"I'm learning that sometimes an activity is restful, and at other times it becomes work. For instance, baking cookies with my granddaughter versus having to bake cookies for an event. However, laundry rarely makes the restful category!"

After lunch with my old friends, we each repeat our salutations before leaving the restaurant, sensing our impromptu lunch was providential. By keeping Sabbath in context, we drive away feeling full, not just from eating, but from enjoying friendship free from the tyranny of the clock. And guess what? I met my writing goals despite "wasting" time with girlfriends. I would've missed a divine connection as a Sabbatarianist, but God knows I function best when I'm flexible.

Ahyana is a single young professional who travels often for work. The first time her reply to one of my letters slipped through my inbox, she was sending me a prayer request. Life plans suddenly unraveled and she was feeling desperate. In a valiant effort, she choked back tears, quietly typed an email while her household slept, and sent it to me. Brave trust began the first of many exchanges between us. We don't know each other in the flesh, but I know this: she believes that prayer changes things. She writes with another brave admission about letting go of uncertainty as she practices Sabbath:

The only way I have been able to let go is letting others in by allowing them to see, hear, and know that I don't have it all together. Gaining weight, I started a vicious cycle of exercising, limiting foods, and self-loathing—again. I was starting to spend more than I was saving. Attending church regularly, but overdosing on trying to become as spiritually enlightened as possible by signing up for as many classes as my schedule would permit. My once firm boundaries with various people were starting to go from solid to Jell-O. Unhealthy dynamics were slowly permeating my life. I was still praying fervently, earnestly, desperately. In fact, I said to God once, It's me, Ahyana; the h is silent. I prayed that prayer as I sat in church sobbing.

Shortly after that prayer, Ahyana felt a gentle touch on her shoulder and discovered a woman was praying for her. As her breathing became less labored, the stranger asked how she could pray specifically. And Ahyana took the risk and let her in. The more she allowed people into her pain, she discovered how self-reliance was keeping her from Sabbath rest:

It's been these examples of other believers partnering with me through difficulties that allow me to say I can rest; I can Sabbath. I can release guilt over not being available for twenty-four hours when a friend or family member has a meltdown. I can let go of worry about revising my résumé for the umpteenth time, thinking this one will maximize my potential and gifts, assuring a new job or promotion.

Ahyana knows Sabbath is *about* God, but only through allowing herself to trust others, did she learn that Sabbath is being *with* God. Rest and love are connected:

For me, resting, releasing, and Sabbath-keeping has been intimately linked with trust. The more my trust grows, the more I can release and rest. I know God has my back. In the context of healthy relationships with other believers and building a support network, I have learned to release and surrender to the God of the Sabbath.

When we feel unloved, we tend to push, hurry, and hustle. When we feel loved with nothing to prove, we enter rest more easily. In Sabbath, we become our truest self. In the same way leaves let go of branches, we understand God's intent in the fourth commandment by letting go of expectations; we allow the process of transition to shape a Sabbath heart and birth a new season. He gives hints he is near during the uncomfortable unknowns in transitions, but often we assume the hints are random and inconsequential—the curious smell of baby powder permeating outdoor space, a stranger offering empathy at just the right moment, and for my friend Laura, the process of buying a house.

As a teen mom, Laura learned early how to rely on God for the basic needs in life. As her daughter grew into a teenager, Laura married for the first time, becoming pregnant with her second daughter shortly thereafter. As a new family, the process of buying their first home together causes a crisis of trust. She unpacks the revelation with me in a letter:

> God doesn't answer my prayers the way I want, but he still answers! That is such a huge revelation for me. I did not even realize I didn't believe God listened to my prayers. I have always felt more like my prayers were desperate attempts to ask and just see if God would help. Awful, I know.
>
> Buying this house is also showing me the depths of my fears. When I first started looking for a house, I told the Realtor, no house on a major thoroughfare. Well, of course, this house is on a busy street. I have huge abandonment issues and fear my daughter will get hurt. Despite my fears, my husband and I decided just to look at it, and of course it was the most beautiful home among all the others we toured. I cried out to God, "Why do you always seem to give me my dreams with a twist? A beautiful home on the edge of danger?"

Laura goes on to tell me she begins having nightmares about her daughter missing in the new house, wandering into the street. The fear of uncertainty takes up residence in her subconscious and she reaches out to me for prayer. The more she surrenders the fear to God, the more she hears the truth. She is worthy of the dream house without a twist. What seemed like second-best through the lens of fear, she discovers, is actually a miracle picked out especially for her family. Resting in God brings clarity and peace, she writes:

A few days ago, I had another dream that we were building a beautiful fence around the front of the house. My heart is starting to trust more deeply. The hardest part about Sabbath for me is that a lot of the time, when I try to rest in God, I hear nothing but crickets. I know the block in my heart is because he wants me to learn that he really does love me. It's so much easier to stay busy on Sabbath than face the fear that I may only hear crickets. But after realizing this week that God really does see and hear me, I know he loves me and now I can rest.

In the same way Laura struggles with trust during a new season of parenting, my mother's heart grows incrementally anxious with each day that passes when I think about the consequences of moving my teenage son to Europe.

Seated across from Harrison, just the two of us at dinner, a lone candle flickers in the middle of the table. After cutting a roll and filling it with barbecued pork, he builds a story between bites, revealing dreams I hadn't heard him speak of before.

As we debrief about the day's events and homework, he explains a longing to board a ship and sail to Europe so he can attend school in the UK and live in a small flat. A new home, overlooking the city, where he can watch people bustling about. "I don't want to live with regrets," he says with a half-smile, eyes squinting behind his hipster glasses. In essence, what my son is expressing is that he doesn't want to live chasing someone else's dream for his life. H and I hadn't mentioned our dream to live in London yet. This new awareness becomes a holy moment over dinner at 6:30 on a Wednesday night. Nodding my head, I assure Harrison that his dad and I want him to live with abandon.

He continues, "I would rather live a meager existence than be trapped by expectations, sitting behind a desk of conformity. I want to live free to express myself, not constrained by time and a desk." Maybe he expects to witness shock written on my face or hear the typical motherly response. But I know I have a choice in this moment: a choice about loving my son for who he is, with trust in God's providence, or allowing the fear of uncertainty a stronghold. His dreams don't scare me for a lack of concrete security, because I see myself reflected in his convictions.

"More than anything else, I want you to be friends with Jesus," I tell him, "because he has created you with purpose, and as long as you are communicating with him, I am sure your life will be fulfilling."

My mother's heart swoons with joy about the confidence and vision I hear growing in my boy. But more than that, divulging dreams about moving to Europe are a holy confirmation. While H and I walk around with swollen hearts for England, God is preparing Harrison for change too, even though he isn't aware of the imminent changes about to happen.

In that moment of divine dinner conversation, I could've admitted to my yearnings about England, made a big deal about the serendipity, squashed idealism with real-life experience, and steered the conversation toward my preferred outcome. But God doesn't rush in like a bulldozer; he allows the Holy Spirit to woo us gently. I knew those moments were sacred. Instead of allowing my overzealous in-the-moment personality to lead as usual, I let go and trusted God with the process. When I brought up the conversation later, Harrison didn't remember it. That's why I wrote down the details that night in my journal. I didn't want to pass over the way God cared for my mother's heart and later regret not recording it on paper.

For us, a leap of faith means letting go of the need for certainty. Though experienced in ruthless trust with eight moves previously, this one is different. We have teenagers now, including a daughter of the age requiring a separate visa to live in another country.

And obtaining a visa to work in England will be a small miracle after layers of bureaucracy. All the *how, what, when* questions are unanswerable in this scenario.

Scary?

Risky?

Unconventional?

Crazy?

Yes. Yes. Yes. And yes.

I am borrowing bravery and learning how to trust from Abraham in the account of the sacrificial binding of Isaac (known as the *Akedah* in Hebrew). God said, "Take your son, your only son, whom you love—Isaac—and go to the region of Moriah. Sacrifice him there as a burnt offering on a mountain I will show you" (Genesis 22:2).

Abraham got up early, saddled his donkey, prepared his servants to travel, and split wood for the offering. Three days later, the mountain they were walking toward appeared in the distance. And can I just stop right there and assume he got a huge pit in his stomach and lump in his throat? But then, Abraham says something that reveals the depth of his trust. He told his two young servants, "Stay here with the donkey while I and the boy go over there. We will worship and then we will come back to you" (22:5).

We is the key word here. Not *I*, but *we*. Even in the midst of all that uncertainty about how things were going to go down, Abraham is sure he will return with Isaac. He doesn't know how, but he trusts beyond comprehension. "God will see to it that there's a sheep for the burnt offering" (22:8 MSG).

Abraham named that place *God-Yireh* or "God-see-to-it." God sees to our uncertainty with his power, presence, and majesty. In Abraham's case, just as he was about to plunge a knife into his son, an angel called out to him by name. And Abraham's response? "Yes, I'm listening."

There are many days and many weeks when I approach Sabbath the same way Abraham approached the *Akedah*. I don't know how I am going to insert rest into my life, but God will show me if I listen to him. He has a track record for providing what we need when we need it and sometimes in ways beyond comprehension.

It's easy to find solace in someone's story of pain and overcoming hardship as a comfort to your misery. But what about when it is you living the story? Well, that requires a whole new level of brave trust and putting faith into action. Mostly, living a good story requires listening attentively like Abraham shows us. Imagine if Abraham had poor recall, without a clue how to distinguish the angel of God speaking from his inner dialogue in that crucial moment (see Genesis 22:11–12). When Abraham looked up, he saw a ram struggling in the thicket; rescue was right there waiting for him.

Over the next few months, H and I sit our kids down and tell them how God is leading us on a faith journey to London. And the first thing my daughter asks? "Who gets the flat screen television?" She isn't upset, dejected, or worried we are leaving her; she's thinking through practical details about how our overseas move will affect her. And Harrison? He's excited about the possibilities of attending a British school.

We meet with friends, intercessors, and leaders whom we respect and the miraculous begins to unfold. H takes Harrison on another scouting trip to London. Open doors, extravagant favor, all confirmations that we had indeed heard God accurately. We weren't crazy after all. Or were we?

Those early signs translated as permission to begin deconstructing life as we'd known it for a dozen years while living in the coastal south. The arduous undertaking of preparing for an overseas move meant sorting through decades of memories and excess, sacrificing an attic full of keepsakes and making plans to sell most of our furniture. We discard 30 percent of the material possessions proving our history together and pack the remainder in cardboard boxes labeled in bold black marker: *ENGLAND* or *STORAGE*. All the while, we're preparing Murielle for her first year of college.

We don't have a new address yet. The only predictable aspect of our lives is a Sabbath rhythm. And week after week, Sabbath becomes our lamb in the thicket.

Like Abraham, our ears were fine-tuned for the *GO,* fueled with anticipation. "Go from your country, your people and your father's household to the land I will show you" (Genesis 12:1). Abraham's story was comforting my fear of uncertainty with a hopeful ending.

Then God sobered us with perspective.

When the timeline for our departure wasn't as concrete as we thought, unexpected delays in a bureaucratic process threatened to incapacitate me with worry. Joy about what God seemed to be unfolding for us turned into desperate, tearful clinging to prayers of intercessors for guidance. My need for security in finances, relationships, home, job title, and influence were overriding my faith in a loving Father. I longed for certainty in our future more than I longed for Jesus.

That little revelation was my undoing as well as a new beginning.

In the stifling August heat, instead of boarding a plane to England as anticipated, so Harrison could start British school, we load our minivan and once again drive twenty-two hours north to the place of belonging—our family cottage in Canada. Sabbath was my only prescription for the relief of heaviness overtaking my entire being.

The first day at the cottage, I awakened in the same garage suite where I first heard that curious word *writ.* I pulled back the curtains to view the lake and was welcomed by a gray bowl of cloud cover, rain spitting on the windows. Instead of taking a sunny walk with my camera, I climbed back in bed with a stack of books. H picked up his phone, uncharacteristically scanning emails. We were like kids anticipating our first trip to Disney World, waiting for someone to tell us, "Today is the day you're going to know when you'll begin the adventure." We needed something firm, concrete, a word of confirmation so hope could finally launch. But instead, H was told what we already suspected; he was short-listed for a job as the vicar of a church in London with an undetermined timeline regarding the process. More waiting.

I began throwing books across the room, while tears streamed down my face. I wasn't sad, I was angry. How will we pay our bills when H's salary runs out in a couple of weeks? When do we put our house up for sale? What about Harrison? What will he do when the school year starts? We don't want to enroll him in school in the U.S. if we're going to be leaving for the UK a few weeks later. How will it affect him to start a British school late? How will we pay tuition for our daughter's first year of university?

The weather, along with the email, to me felt like God was being mean-spirited. I wanted to run away, but there was nowhere I could go and be away from Jesus. I questioned, *Is God purposely withholding a blessing?*

Slowly, my will to keep believing in the unseen and "not yet" trickled out like a tire with a tiny hole in it. On the outside, no one knew my faith was collapsing. I wonder if God knows me so well; surely he knows my capacity is diminishing. *Why isn't he doing something to rescue us from this situation?*

After breakfast, I retreat back in the quiet garage suite with a cup of warm tea cupped in my hands, drawn to open *Sacred Echo* by Margaret Feinberg on my Kindle, a book I was prompted to purchase before we left on our trip, when I couldn't find the hard copy on our bookshelves. A few paragraphs into the first chapter, my eyes land on words making my heart beat fast and my spine straighten:

> God's wisdom and instruction are more than info-to-go. When we view God as just a source of information, then our understanding of him becomes myopic and we forget that God's words are not merely words, but life to be ingested. They nourish our souls. And he is the source of all life. When we focus on mere information, we lose touch with the reality that God's words contain unfathomable power.[3]

Conviction tells me that I have misinterpreted relationship with my heavenly Father. In the context of uncertainty about the future,

I've treated our conversations as a fast-food option for the list of unknowns hungry for resolution. I am empty, unfulfilled, and yet addicted to needing assurance every time a possible solution is thwarted.

And then Margaret's wisdom continues based on a verse in Hosea: "'He will come to us like the winter rains, like the spring rains that water the earth' (Hosea 6:3). Spring rain is not just an idea, but a wet experience in awakening, redemption, and restoration that cleanses and brings new life. I ache for God's love to be more than an intellectual assertion in my life. I long to be flooded with his love."[4]

Me, too. I could say it with humility and deep conviction. In those few moments of restful quiet, stilling my heart and waiting, Peace came flooding over me when I listened to the nudge about opening a book and reading words lying in my lap. God even cares about how I interpret the weather.

Closing my eyes in prayerful repentance, I hear a whisper in response to my silent meditation: *The church needs as much resolve in choosing you to be at the church as you have about moving to England. I'm not making you wait because I don't love you, but because I love everyone involved in the process. I know timing is crucial for Harrison. I want him to know that I have something in this move for him too. He isn't going to London just because he has to or because he is tagging along to your calling. I have purpose in it for him as well. The circumstances will reveal that to him. You told Harrison to be thinking about other people when he makes decisions, but you aren't doing that yourself. You must be mindful of how this decision affects more than just you. There are a lot of other people this will affect. I'm at work here. It's not that I don't love you, it's because I do—that you must continue to wait.*

Tears stream down my face again, but this time, not from anger. The tears represent thankfulness and awe over God's steadfast love in spite of my lack of faith. A few minutes later, H waltzes back into the suite assuming my red, swollen face is a sign of contempt until he witnesses the sheepish smile spreading across my lips. I tell him about my encounter, what I sense God is saying, and H admits it's a confirmation to his private prayers earlier that morning.

"I feel that God is actually giving me a vision for the church. I know this may sound crazy," he admits.

I often expect answers to prayers like a farmer laying down tracks with big wheels between rows of plants—I expect straightforward, direct, clear, and predictable response. But God doesn't promise easy answers; he promises he will be with us. More than just knowing about his love, Jesus longs for us to encounter his love.

Fear looks for assurance when certainty is fallow. For me, assurance looks like scrolling through social media feeds to numb anxiety, polling friends for opinions that affirm my fear is warranted, and surveying the best options. The longer the silence of unknowns, the more I walk around asking, "What do you want me to do?" And God responds, "Be with me."

If I do less, I am not less. If you do less, you are not less. Fear of uncertainty communicates the opposite. Our need for certainty silences the still, small voice—what many refer to as intuition—that knower in your gut that says it is time to stop, listen, abide, rest, Sabbath. Sabbath stilling is an intimate pause declaring "I love you" in response to the myriad different ways he's communicated love to us during the other six days of the week.

In somewhat the same way God tested Abraham on the climb up the mountain as he pondered the *Akedah* (though not nearly as costly), this grievous interruption on our way to London is God testing us with the same question: *Are you using me for what you want or trusting me to use you to fulfill my ultimate purposes?*

I'm learning that when we say yes to God and let go of the need for certainty, that doesn't mean he'll grant our every wish or provide rescue with instant security. God cares more about our transformation into his image than immediate relief. His plans are good and often broader than we imagine. Over time, this truth transforms my addiction to certainty into a craving for the intimacy I experience with Jesus on Sabbath. One day of rest, which

I initially interpreted as a sacrifice, becomes the day to remember how deeply I am loved.

Like Abraham arriving at Mount Moriah, we have not arrived at this place waiting for the revelation of providence without years of working out our salvation by surrender and testing. When your only choice is to pray, trust, and accept plunging the knife into the dreams you've held tightly, God will provide rescue, a glimmer of hope through a ram in the thicket. We must die to life as we know it for resurrection to take place. That's what H and I were doing while we were waiting to move to London, though we weren't fully aware of the consequences the day we boarded that flight in Dallas.

CHAPTER TEN

Preparation Is Everything

We crave balance, but need rhythm.

Mark Buchanan, *Spiritual Rhythms*

The sun is low, warming my skin like standing close to an open fire on a cold evening—comforting, cozy, and somehow healing.

Day eight of our two weeks at the cottage becomes the second day of warm weather since arriving. When the first week is a memory scribed in my journal, we begin counting the days left of our vacation with a backdrop of dread. We don't want the slow Sabbath days to end.

Wading slowly into a glassy bowl of warm lake water, mud squishes between my toes with each step toward the drop-off. When my neck submerges underwater, I inspect dragonflies floating on the surface, spinning my arms slowly left, then right, making small ripples without moving the core of my body. As I relish the few undisturbed moments, a childhood memory emerges. A time with my grandparents at a lake in the hills of Missouri, when seaweed roped around ankles, sending shudders up to my elbows in slimy awareness of a mystery lying in the deep. Grandma practiced the sidestroke wearing a rubber swim cap, appliquéd flowers fluttering in the breeze. Water was always too cold for Grandpa, no matter how intensely the sun blazed. He dozed on the beach, waving at intervals in response to the sound of my small voice calling for him. Braunschweiger and mayo sandwiches with handfuls of Bugles from the picnic basket, washed down with canned soda—and the outhouse crawling with daddy longlegs—these fragmented memories of fond childhood summers echo in my mind. In the recollection, I realize how those sleepy summer days were preparation for wading into the lake now as an adult, navigating a new faith journey.

Sabbath is my modus operandi at the cottage, an easy posture when choices are limited and schedules empty, void of responsibility. What about the seasons of life overflowing, with crowds elbowing their way to the front of lines? We're all a bit star struck with returning to busyness in September.

Preparation is everything. I wrote that phrase to the Sabbath Society in a weekly letter regarding the practical aspects of making Sabbath-keeping successful—experiencing the fullness of rest by focusing fully on the details of living a full life. Making preparation in the mundane details of life primes a heart for abiding well, and most important, below the surface. When Jesus asks, "What do you want me to do for you?" preparation is everything too.

If I'm unprepared to answer his earnest question, then how do I know where life is taking me? "Time is a relentless river," writes Ann Voskamp:

> It rages on, a respecter of no one. And this is the only way to slow time: When I fully enter time's swift current, enter into the current moment with the weight of all my attention, I slow the torrent with the weight of me all here. I can slow the torrent by being all here. I only live the full life when I live fully in the moment.[1]

I have to think that the women who traveled with Jesus from Galilee were fully in the moment the day they saw the tomb and how his body was laid in it. It was Preparation Day, and the Sabbath was about to begin.

Luke doesn't tell us that the women wept in grief or about the empathy they expressed in shared conversation. We are left within the limits of our imagination as to how they processed the pain of the crucifixion. No, he tells us they went home and prepared spices and perfumes for Jesus' burial. And then they rested on Sabbath in obedience to the commandment (see Luke 23:54–56).

Their preparation was an act of love and their rest an act of faith.

Preparing isn't as much about what we do as it is about creating space for expectancy. Preparation in rest precedes the miracle. When we run errands early in the week, clean up the house, prepare food for the weekend, these are acts of love at the root. Preparing for Sabbath communicates to Jesus, "You matter most. I want to spend time with you." And rest on a day filled with uncertainty, like it was for the women from Galilee, is an act of faith overriding rational thought. A faith that communicates, "I trust that what you say is true."

Because the women were prepared, Luke tells us that they arose early to find the stone rolled away from Jesus' tomb. They got up early because they were expectant about being with him, and therefore the first to witness the miracle of the resurrection. Revelation comes more quickly with rest.

I may be dreading the days ahead, but I wade into the unknowns trusting the mysteries of Christ are hidden in the deep places of abiding with him.

"They saw the works of the Lord, his wondrous deeds in the deep" (Psalm 107:24), and we can trust Jesus with our time because he has a track record of reliability and generosity, even when the boundaries he places on us are sometimes uncomfortable. In Sabbath, we are reminded that the lines have fallen for us in pleasant places, even when the lines are narrow (see Psalm 16:6).

Sabbath is a narrowing; a limit, a boundary, a tight passageway that requires shedding all the excess baggage hindering us from entering fully into his rest.[2] We attempt to set ourselves free from limits, but God uses them for our good. "I have seen a limit to all perfection, but your commandment is exceedingly broad" (Psalm 119:96 ESV).

If the fourth commandment is broad and spacious, can we embrace narrow seasons with limitations as God's best for the moment in the same way a day of rest for the women who waited to prepare his body was God's best? Narrow seasons, such as parenting young children and serving people on Sunday, limit time for rest. The thought of choosing Sabbath can make us feel even more hemmed in and off-balance. In the seasons of life beholden by limitations, rest seems an impossibility unless we approach time with faith and trust—faith that God's commandment to remember the Sabbath and keep the day holy isn't exclusive language. "The fear of the Lord is the beginning of wisdom; all those who practice it have a good understanding" (Psalm 111:10 ESV). Choose to believe that repentance and rest is your salvation, "in quietness and in trust shall be your strength" (Isaiah 30:15).

When I am fully aware of clouds moving, birds trilling, insects buzzing, and downy feathers floating on the still lake, I lean into the portal from this moment, beyond next week, and into the grand scale of things, weighing the collection of meaningful moments holding my life together. He is continually in the process of preparing us for the future he envisions. We obtain hope to move forward into the spacious place of Sabbath when we realize there are no limitations to his presence, power, purpose, and pleasure when we invite him to join us in the narrow places.

"Preparation is everything. Absolutely. Living with an eye toward preparation rather than survival is a dying art," writes Natalie,

Right now, when it comes to Sabbath, I just stop, unless of course, I can't. You know, "I can't" meaning the in-laws are here or something major is happening on Monday or it's the

week I start directing the play or. . . . It's easy to avoid stopping. Preparation would help me whittle down the "I can't" situations even more. This comes down to rhythm, and mine is slowly being built in, including adding some extra kitchen prep to my Saturday morning. One of the biggest hurdles for me right now is preparing for the week mentality in terms of details and planning. But I did have a wonderful moment. I was looking at my to-do app for today and saw a notice that said, "Nothing due tomorrow." Practice makes progress.

Two nights before sinking my toes into silty water, my family sits close under blankets around a campfire and beneath starry skies. We're practicing awe when Murielle asks questions about my past she never thought to utter before. Questions spill out safely when there is margin for answers. She asks me about university, choosing a major, my brave cross-country move from Oklahoma, and meeting her dad in Arizona. And aren't we all storytellers, waiting for the opportunity to prepare someone fresh on a faith journey?

H stokes the fire, and the sky bleeds from slate into charcoal and pools ebony while conversations careen carelessly from stages of maturing into facts about stars, planets, and constellations. Harrison interjects, "Did you know the Milky Way has a black center?"

"Yes," I replied, "it's full of Milky Way candy bars."

Murielle giggles and silliness become contagious for all of us sitting around the campfire.

Cousins squeeze into the gaps of conversation once their little people are tucked into bed and snoring. Noah begins teasing H about the way he picks up accents easily, wondering if he will pick up an English accent in London. "You can hardly say the Lord's Prayer without saying, 'Our Fautha,'" admits H.

"Murielle will call home and say, 'What happened to my family?!'" chides Noah. And laughter erupts in unison.

Later, while we're fluffing pillows and closing windows for the evening, H remarks, "I don't remember the last time we had a conversation like that with the kids; I loved it."

I smile in agreement. Our imminent move to England has sparked something back to life in the kids. Sabbath days huddled in close with loved ones provide a safe haven, fueling dreams and visions.

Our ability to envision the future is mental preparation for what lies ahead, whether tomorrow, next week, or years in the future, and it is a needed discipline for making rhythms of rest realistic. But what if all you envision is the reality of mundane life pressed in all around you and the longing for rest unreachable?

Becky writes,

> To be honest, my heart has said "I'm all in" when it comes to Sabbath, but I haven't figured out how to practically implement the change in my life. In this season of raising little ones while balancing ministry, a part-time job, writing, and trying to keep everyone fed and clothed, I just don't know how to cut things out, to slow down.

In the same way a quiet campfire conversation kindles my daughter's questions, Becky is stoking the weekly email conversation toward the work of preparation for Sabbath. As a newcomer, she is curious and eager to learn from others with more experience. I invite everyone to add their wisdom on her behalf. A veteran to the group, Alee, responds first with an echo to what many are learning the more they practice rest as a rhythm of life:

> The first thing I would share with newcomers is this: Sabbath is not going to look like you think it should. It's not going to be anything that you are expecting it to be. It will be difficult, wonderful, enlightening, refreshing, and restorative, but not exactly what you are expecting. Be encouraged that the transition is more than worth it. You will discover a deeper and richer view of your life, God, and the world.

Idealism is the thief of Sabbath. And the voice of idealism in Sabbath sounds like this: I will take a day off to rest when I get everything done or when I'm in a different season of life or when I have another vocation, or, my least favorite voice from the crowd: when I'm retired. Sabbath isn't about resting perfectly; it's about resting in the One who is perfect. A Sabbath heart asks, "How can I embrace my limits? Am I willing to let go of whatever God is asking me to shed? Can I see how God uses narrowing my time as his will for the moment?"

Self-help and how-to resources are plentiful on themes surrounding a balanced life. We all want five easy steps to free us from tiredness and chaos, but our attempts end up like a New Year's resolution. Two weeks into good intentions, expectancy dissolves into disappointment when we fail to meet up to those unrealistic standards.

❦ ❦ ❦

I'm going to stop here and share something potentially life altering. Are you ready for it? Paying attention? Focused? Here goes: There is no such thing as balance.

I know. It's profound, even revolutionary. You're going to highlight that sentence and tweet about it. People will follow you in droves. Of course, I'm being sarcastic. The truth is, in order for anything to shift from a "should" to a "joy," from a practice to a lifestyle, and from novice to expert, requires an intentional, focused, and disciplined life. But there are no perfect solutions, no simple set of steps to follow to achieve a state of perfection in ordering the days of your life. However, there is a difference between being purposeful and being driven about time.

In the fifth chapter of *The Rest of God*, Mark Buchanan points out that Jesus lived with the highest and clearest purpose, yet he veered and strayed from one distraction to the next with no apparent plan.

"Who touched me?" (Luke 8:45)

"You give them something to eat." (Mark 6:37)

"Let's go over to the other side." (Luke 8:22)

Can you imagine Jesus saying, "I don't have time for that, I've got to get to Jerusalem"?

Buchanan says, "Pay attention to how God is afoot in the mystery of each moment, in its mad rush or maddening pool. He is present in all that."[3]

I might add, see how he is afoot on the Internet. More than managing time, I want to pay more attention to the minutes I'm given. To have an "inner ear for the Father's whispers, a third eye for the Spirit's motions" in work, my inboxes, conversations, and relationships near and online, on social media feeds, and in times of rest.

When we see time as a generous gift of invitation instead of something we hoard selfishly, we are more generous with the hours given us and free from the tyranny of the urgent. In "giving away" twenty-four hours to rest and pay attention, he seems to bless what is initially considered a sacrifice, in the same way he blesses finances in tithing. When I give time away to God first, I have the capacity to give myself and resources away to others joyfully. I realize time spent for the sake of someone else isn't time wasted at all. He redeems what I often consider a sacrifice.

In the classic story of *Black Beauty*, Jerry, the horse's owner, faces a dilemma about altering his six-day cab license in order to take Mrs. Briggs, a client, to church on Sunday. Caring for the needs of his wife, Mr. Briggs implores, "It is very proper that every person should have rest, and be able to go to church on Sundays, but I should have thought you would not have minded such a short distance for the horse, and only once a day; you would have all the afternoon and evening for yourself, and we are very good customers, you know."[4]

Mr. Briggs is an echo of that bossy inner voice attempting to muddy good intentions. My "boss" has a familiar voice, provoking inner conflict. Maybe it has a convincing cadence for you too.

My heart yearns for quiet time, but the boss says, *You should get the laundry folded and the dishes done or you'll be behind on Monday. Just this one load,* I think, and a few minutes later, I'm rearranging closets.

Pulling weeds is therapeutic, but the boss slyly convinces, *That whole patch of the garden should be reworked, it looks terrible.* As the sun recedes into twilight, instead of feeling rejuvenated by basking in nature, I'm exhausted from attempting to conquer a patch of earth. "We are not what we can conquer, but what is given to us," Henri Nouwen wisely writes.[5]

Cooking is a creative outlet, but the boss implores, *You should make one more batch of cookies or one more side dish for dinner in case there isn't enough food for the weekend.* What begins as a joyful endeavor changes into the fear of scarcity and an excess of dirty dishes.

"Come to me, all you who are weary and burdened, and I will give you rest," Jesus says in the book of Matthew (11:28). Heavy laden is often the result of listening to the *shoulds* of the bossy inner voice that degrades passion into duty and joy into meaninglessness. When peace disintegrates into a dull ache of anxiety, Jesus offers a solution: "Take my yoke upon you and learn from me, for I am gentle and humble in heart, and you will find rest for your souls. For my yoke is easy and my burden is light" (Matthew 11:29–30).

Easy and *light*: Two words to use as a guideline when you are tempted to break your resolve to rest. First, ask yourself this question: Is what I'm considering easy and does it make me feel light? If the answer is no, then you know you are being bullied.

Jerry's response to Mr. Briggs' offer reveals freedom in rest from a place of wholehearted lightness, when he says, "I can't give up Sundays, sir, indeed I can't. I read that God made man, and he made horses and the other beasts, and as soon as He had made them He made a day of rest, and bade that all should rest one day in seven; and I think, sir, He must have known what was good for them, and I am sure it is good for me; I am stronger and healthier altogether, now that I have a day of rest; the horses are fresh too, and do not wear out nearly so fast. The six-day drivers all tell me the same, and I have laid by more money in the savings bank than ever I did before; and as for the wife and children, sir, why, hearts alive! They would not go back to the seven days for all they could see."

Perhaps your boss is wagging her finger across an upturned nose, attempting to woo you away from Sabbath with temptations. Are you allowing the "shoulds" to boss you around? When it comes to the ways in which you approach Sabbath, don't allow compromise of inner conflict to take up residence. Stay strong in your convictions. Sabbath DNA is unique to each of us.

Mark Buchanan says this is "Sabbath's golden rule: Cease from what is necessary. Embrace that which gives life."[6] How does this golden rule look to you, practically speaking?

I spend a large number of hours writing on my computer during the week, so I don't allow myself to open the computer on Sabbath because writing feels more like work. For me, compromise sounds like, *Oh, go ahead; one little paragraph won't hurt.* But for you, writing may be a restful luxury to dip into.

I may take a walk with my camera as a way to enjoy the outdoors. But when a walk becomes about exercise with a preferred outcome, like burning calories to shed pounds, I've slipped into compromise that desecrates Sabbath.

Organizing a drawer or closet can often be a rejuvenating activity until it is a mess I feel I have to clean up before I can rest easy. When I ask myself if the activity is easy and if it makes me feel lighter, my answer determines how I choose to spend time on Sabbath.

Once we ran out of milk on Sabbath. Nonetheless, we managed to avoid the grocery store and survived just fine without it. Often what seems necessary in the moment can often wait, making way for a day that is holy, set apart, and different.

Further in the story of *Black Beauty*, Jerry applies the Golden Rule when he is faced with a hard decision. Dinah, a friend, is in need of transport to reach her dying mother, but Jerry is tired and so are the horses. He doesn't want to give up his Sunday, but his wife, Polly, offers wisdom. Perhaps you can relate? "I am sure it won't break the Sabbath, for if pulling a poor beast or donkey out of a pit would not spoil it, I am quite sure taking poor Dinah would not do it."[7]

As the story goes, Dinah's family lives in a small farmhouse on a beautiful meadow, where Jerry and his horse, Jack, find the unexpected gift of respite. After returning home, Jerry's first words were, "Well, Polly, I have not lost my Sunday after all, for the birds were singing hymns in every bush, and I joined in the service; and as for Jack, he was like a young colt."[8]

We learn from Jerry in the story of *Black Beauty* about paying attention to how God is afoot in the mystery of each moment. When the day we choose to Sabbath is interrupted or unusually active, we can trust God for redemption in rest. With practice, over time, we achieve a Sabbath heart and resolve remains steadfast whatever the context.

A letter from Sheila offers a real-life example. She writes,

Thought of you yesterday (Sunday) as I was preparing an impromptu anniversary dinner for my sister-in-law and her husband. We didn't know that they were coming until Saturday afternoon, when we were headed out for graduation parties. Even then, we didn't know if they would stay long enough for lunch. So, Betty Crocker helped me out with potatoes, Birds Eye mixed fancy veggies, baked chicken breasts, fresh veggie & pickle tray, and real whipped cream on fresh brownies with raspberries on top. Not really much fuss, and did for their wedding anniversary this week. Good conversation with extended family. And it felt like an offering to God for family—not work. A nice nap after they left about 3:00 helped too. Such a blessing to have freedom in our rest.

One year later, Becky writes me back and her letter puts a smile on my face. Not only does she answer all of her original questions about making Sabbath a reality, she reveals that a rhythm of rest is not only possible but realistic in the throes of parenting little people. It turns out preparation really is everything:

*In the context of practicing Sabbath as a mom of little ones,
I found that making some clear distinctions between Sunday
and the rest of the week was extremely helpful. No, I can't
lie on the couch and read books or spend hours in prayer
or devotion as I'd like to (as I used to think Sabbath should
be,) because kiddos still need my near-constant help and
attention. But I found that even in the midst of mothering,
I could establish some workable parameters that would help
the Sabbath feel set apart.*

Initially, Becky decided there were certain things she *would not* do on Sabbath—dishes, laundry, extensive cooking, opening the computer, engaging in social media, or emailing from her phone. Then she decided there were things she *would* do on Sabbath—nap, read a book while her kids slept, spend intentional time with family by playing a board game or LEGOs, and watching movies together.

These aren't specific rules Becky is making that create a legalistic Sabbath practice, but rather boundaries that allow greater flexibility in rhythms of rest. Becky also works part time from home, and before making Sabbath a lifestyle, Sunday was the day she often caught up on work because her husband was available to look after their young boys. That little detail became her greatest obstacle to rest. How was she going to give up the possibility of working on Sabbath when the rest of the week already felt maxed beyond capacity?

The answer? Intention, planning, and sacrifice.

She prepared ahead of time by getting in enough hours before Sabbath arrived or by waking up early the following Monday or Tuesday to meet a deadline. The same was true with dishes, laundry, and meals. Though she enjoys going to bed with an empty sink, Becky began to relish in the physical break Sabbath afforded her.

She admits,

*At the beginning, it was a stretch. I had to get myself and
my family acclimated to my new routine as well as explain*

again and again why I wasn't going to empty the dishwasher or pick up the toys or make X, Y, or Z for dinner. I even had to unplug and stow my laptop away in a high cupboard to keep myself from running on autopilot and hopping on throughout the day for email or Facebook, recipes, or work. The beginning weeks and months often felt cumbersome and awkward.

But over time I found something remarkable: I looked forward to Sundays with increasing excitement! I got better at planning my week in the areas I needed to be freed up on Sunday to rest. There really was time to get it all done the other six days. And what had to fall by the wayside probably wasn't that important to begin with. More than a sacrifice, Sabbath-keeping started to feel like a gift.

And then Becky echoes Alee's wisdom about letting go of idealism:

The one thing I want moms of little ones to know is my Sabbath doesn't always feel super spiritual. Yet I know for certain that resting is a spiritual act of worship, and God is using it to transform my heart. I have more space in my spirit, mind, and body to listen and respond to the Spirit, not only on Sundays but throughout the week. Practicing Sabbath has been huge in minimizing that feeling that so many young moms like me have of just going, going, going without a break. I'm still a mom on Sundays, but pausing from some of the regular to-dos helps me remember that I'm a human being, not a human doing. God cares for who I am, not just what I do for my family, and it's okay—nay, necessary—to take time to remember that and allow the Lord to minister to my heart. And sometimes He does that through a long nap and frozen pizza on paper plates.

Several in the seasons with narrow margins for rest write to me with an echo: Planning ahead, organizing details, and thinking through priorities all lead to a rich and realistic (not perfect) Sabbath rhythm.

Ann Voskamp teaches, "The parent must always self-parent first, self-preach before child-teach, because who can bring peace unless they've held their own peace? Christ incarnated in the parent is the only hope of incarnating Christ in the child."⁹ And isn't this true in the context of Sabbath-keeping with children? If we choose Sabbath as a day that is set apart, a freedom to be embraced, a gift we look forward to opening every week, aren't we incarnating rest as a lifestyle within our children too? Life spins with responsibilities, but with a Sabbath heart as the axis, an overflow of expectancy from the riches of rest spills out daily through the practice of preparation.

As the home educator of four young children, Kris illustrates what Ann teaches:

We have built into our days the sanctuary of quiet time, which translates as a mini-Sabbath for my children. For me, those translate as my office hours as a work-at-home mom. My children understand the concept of settling down for a period of time. They have learned to be comfortable with quiet, unforced stillness. I can't tell you how many times I've released them only to find them resting quietly, listening to an audiobook, drawing, or napping. At their ages, I have been able to explain God's purpose for Sabbath and they understand that in some ways, it mirrors our rhythm of quiet time.

Because our schedule is what it is, for me, rest is elusive every day of the week except Sunday. Sabbath often sustains me as the week winds down and my own weariness presses in. I always look forward to what Sabbath affords me in an extended quiet time, reading books, writing, or just sitting with my family while we watch a movie. I think when your arms are full of toddlers and preschoolers, Sabbath can seem like an unaffordable luxury, and so it gets ignored, even as we are burning both ends of the candle with exhaustion.

Looking back, I wish I had embraced Sabbath earlier in life; I wish too that I had made it a priority when my children were smaller and the days bled together in a mad dash. I wish I hadn't lived so many years in survival mode.

It may surprise you when I divulge that H and I Sabbath differently. Just because I am the wife of a clergy husband doesn't mean his responsibilities are mine or our rhythms are a mirror image. H and I support each other wholeheartedly, but our gifts and callings are unique. We don't impose work on each other because we are committed to relationship first, and the same goes with how we approach rest. Since those initial uncomfortable days of making rest a weekly rhythm, H and the kids have supported my decision with respect. And we hold each other accountable.

Even though H normally rests from work on Friday, his day off, it's not uncommon for him to ask me what I'm doing if he sees me slipping into work on Sunday, the day I choose to Sabbath. He cautions me in a loving way by reminding me that the day is about not doing anything like productive work. And sometimes I need to be caught when I slip up. If I have a busy week, he considers what we need for the weekend, helps curate grocery lists, and runs errands in preparation. Over time and with practice, I've learned to ask for help too.

One of the most productive things you can do toward cultivating peace in Sabbath is to admit when you need help. Being vulnerable can feel scary, but it is the bravest decision we make. When we invite others to participate in what matters most to us, the vulnerability deepens respect. If we are going to be successful at rest, accountability is important. And accountability is easy in Sabbath-keeping when there is an assurance of a good result.

Alee admits the two most difficult aspects of Sabbath-keeping for her family of six is when and how to Sabbath. Initially, everyone was expected to Sabbath on the same day of the week, approaching the day with the same mindset. She says, "In the beginning, there was quite a bit of frustration, which led to several discussions.

All the while, we were discovering what Sabbath looked like for each one of us and how the act of Sabbath would be personally displayed." Over six months of practicing, Alee's family discovered a new freedom. Each person customized the day according to their unique personality and schedule. Two teenage sons, who are athletes, chose Sunday as a day to worship, hang out with friends, and nap, while Alee and her husband chose Saturday to rest. Alee's family found harmony in Sabbath by allowing each person to decide how they wanted to rest, and something amazing happened:

Nowadays, we are more accepting of one another in all aspects of life; more accepting of each other's uniqueness and more open to understanding life from each other's viewpoint. This, of course, is due in part to the luxury of unwrapping Sabbath over time. As we have opened our hearts and minds, God's goodness and His perspective fills each of us and begins to pour out. The process is so natural that we barely notice until we actually pause and evaluate.

Sabbath rhythms infect the atmosphere of the home. As I prepare on Saturday by cooking meals and completing chores, the process becomes a door slowly closing on distractions in order to be fully present with my people. The day is aromatic with anticipation as the kids hover around me in the kitchen, salivating over smells simmering on the stove top and bread baking in the oven. Joy is an undercurrent of Sabbath when we make the day celebratory. And rested people make for a peaceful home.

CHAPTER ELEVEN

L'Chaim! To Life!

Spiritual rest is a journey of awakening our hearts to fully receive.

Bonnie Gray, *Finding Spiritual Whitespace*

Saturdays are saving me.

I'm drawn to the kitchen to create food like a fly to raw meat. This is not the norm for me. In fact, it's downright unusual. When my kids turned into teenagers, and writing became more of a serious endeavor than a casual hobby, cooking mutated into a compulsory chore only when our stomachs signaled our hunger.

But now? The whir of the mixer, the ting of the timer, chocolate melting in the oven, the aroma of chicken simmering in the Crock-Pot—it all seems like a holy union, as if the act of cooking is saving me somehow.

It's been four months since leaving the cottage in Canada, and four months of waiting for a departure date to London. Four months of H waking up without a specific reason for getting dressed in the morning. Four months without an office, a team of people to lead, or a vision to sink our experience into. Four months without a paycheck. News trickles in from London through random emails a few times a week. More silence. More waiting. More of the same. In cooking, I seek some small measure of hope in the mystery that currently encompasses our life.

Four months of roaming around in the wilderness for me, and forty years for the Israelites. Moses reminds us that what enervates in the wilderness, God redeems as preparation for receiving his blessing:

> Remember how the Lord your God led you through the wilderness for these forty years, humbling you and testing you to prove your character, and to find out whether or not you would obey his commands. Yes, he humbled you by letting you go hungry and then feeding you with manna, a food previously unknown to you and your ancestors. He did it to teach you that people do not live by bread alone; rather, we live by every word that comes from the mouth of the Lord.
>
> Deuteronomy 8:2–3 NLT

God is humbling me by allowing us to go hungry, not physically, but in other ways. He is teaching us to rely on the bread of truth for sustenance, to trust that his commandments are good.

Rhythms provide anchoring during the storms of life. And along with rhythms come the manna of ruminating practices—those simple actions that miraculously calm the hurricane of internal processing so we can rest well. He takes what is simple and uses it for our good. Cooking on Saturday has turned out to be one of the ruminating practices that help me trudge through the wilderness. While chopping celery, kneading bread, and making cookie dough, all the things I'm panicked about become settled and contained. Ruminating allows your mind to drift away from the detritus long enough for swirling thoughts to settle with different perspective. Peace and clarity are often the result.

While ruminating, circumstances in the wilderness become the backdrop, and the truth of God's promises move to the forefront.

For some, pulling weeds in the garden is a ruminating practice that allows time to think, assign meaning, and obtain focus. For others, knitting, painting, or a jog around a park brings peace and clear-headed thinking. When we struggle with a lack of inner quiet or find sitting still a miraculous feat, consistently adding a ruminating practice to a Sabbath rhythm can mean that peace—and the truth—will come to mind, spirit, and soul more quickly.

With every delay in our departure to London, I read recipes as if each ingredient may be a clue toward solving speculation about the timeline for moving. In kneading flour with water and oil for challah, I become a perspicacious cook and student of Sabbath. Acknowledging rest is not a recipe with five easy steps, but a re-orientation toward what makes me hungry in the first place. We must rest in order for him to rise within us.

Ruminating overrides my bent to quench thirst for outcomes with my own remedies. Whether encircled on the couch by pencils, markers, and an adult coloring book; meandering with a camera strapped around my neck; or creaming butter and sugar together with a spatula, these simple practices lead me to the ubiquitous sweet aroma of Christ. The mysterious flavor that satiates a hunger for the meaning of life is what draws me back to the kitchen to create on Saturday. I cannot explain how cooking cures lassitude and why I cook with my shoes off. But I do know that the mystery is why we must continue to wait.

Through expectant waiting, I find bread crumbs of his nearness. I write to the Sabbath Society about the trail leading me to hope.

Hello Everyone,

With unexpected delays in our move to England, we've been watching our pennies while we live without income for the past few months. This season makes me grateful for many things I've taken for granted, like a full pantry, meat, and the generosity of others who pay for lunch. Because I like a good challenge, our circumstances allow me to prove my resourcefulness when it comes to planning meals with what we have available.

I'm scouring recipe books that include obscure ingredients stocked behind the familiar items on my pantry shelves. Treasures among the day-old bakery items and carts holding markdowns in the back of the grocery store have become a source of joy. This week, I found one braided loaf of challah mixed in with the muffins and hot dog buns, an unusual find in my beach community.

The challah delivered what I sensed was an invisible epistle from Jesus. A reminder that the items on my grocery list matter to him as much as they do to us. He is our provider and he loves the surprise of unusual gifts.

Challah is yeast-raised egg bread traditionally eaten by Jews on Shabbat. The term challah *refers to a small piece of dough pulled apart and set aside before the dough is braided into a loaf for baking. In biblical times, this small portion was the tithe for Jewish priests (Kohanim).*

In the Jewish tradition, two loaves of challah (challot) are placed on the Sabbath and/or holiday table(s). Two loaves are used in commemoration of the double portion of manna that was provided on Friday to the Israelites in the desert following the Exodus from Egypt (Exodus 16:4–30). The two loaves remind Jews that God will provide for their material needs, even if they refrain from working on the Sabbath day. The loaves are usually covered with a decorative cloth, a reminder of manna falling from the sky and how it was protected by layers of dew.[1] *Before it is eaten, a blessing (HaMotzi) is spoken over the bread.* Blessed are you, Lord our God, King of the universe, who brings forth bread from the earth.

Finding challah is my everyday miracle, the incarnation of Christ meeting me in the grocery store. During this season of lack, I'm finding the kitchen counters are everyday altars of remembrance. In all the unknowns of our uncertain circumstances, the smells simmering on the stove are incense and food, my offering. Saturday has become holy prepara-tion for welcoming Sabbath, a sacredness of time I look forward to often.

> Resting with you,
> *Shelly*

When people ask me how I Sabbath, I know they are hoping for something magical—a list or a technique, like divulging ingre-dients to the best chocolate cake recipe on the planet. But what I'm discovering is the miracle of making Sabbath a reality comes in the mindset.

In the same way cooking for others prepares us to receive people with the spirit of hospitality, the practice of ruminating prepares us to receive God on Sabbath, arms open and extended in welcome.

"My heart continues to turn toward rest, especially in the lat-ter half of the week as I know that Sabbath is coming," writes Kris. "It is a beacon of hope for me, calling me to it. Sabbath has become a much anticipated weekly invitation to stillness, one that I cannot refuse. I know that I can show up just as I am—with my frayed ends and raggedy remains from the week. Sabbath is God patting his lap, and saying, 'Come up here,' like a father does with his children. I am ever more eager to scramble into God's safety and burrow down for a few brief hours."

On Thursday, I clean out my refrigerator, decide on recipes, check the pantry for all the necessary ingredients, and start a gro-cery list for what is missing. I consider the grand scale of weekend activities for the four people under our roof and think through what needs doing through Monday. If I know a busy weekend is an upcoming reality, then a one-pot meal and paper plates or calling up our favorite pizza place is the direction I take. Goals for feeding my family on the weekend are simple: leftovers and a lack of dirty dishes.

Before Sabbath was a priority in planning for the weekend, our days off work were more about time to catch up on responsibilities. Sheila writes me with a similar sentiment:

"When I returned to work as our daughters grew older, it made sense to use Sunday as a catch-up day for laundry, food preparation, or whatever seemed most pressing. Then, a few years ago, I began to experiment with Sabbath rest. The first thing I tried was abstaining from shopping or filling the car with gas. While a seemingly small step, it trained my thought process to keep Sabbath in the forefront of my thinking."

After Sheila completes a Master's degree, she trades study for recreational reading on Sabbath and limits screen time, cultivating a slower pace and quiet mindset. And she becomes more accepting of interruptions on Sabbath: "Sometimes this means welcoming our granddaughters when all I really want is a nap. Or attending a benefit or open house, honoring folks in our neighborhood. But the joy of relationship makes up for the little bit of sleep I might miss."

The incremental changes taught Sheila how to value time differently. She began to utilize the restorative power of silence, and slowly the thrill of marking off tasks from a to-do list lost its luster. "My heart is learning that the important things are completed without constant work and effort. I am learning to rest in the Lord's timing and bask in his presence. And his reward is an inner calm and security that people are beginning to notice."

❦ ❦ ❦

I am asked to write an article for a website on the second chapter of Brett McCracken's book *Gray Matters: Navigating the Space between Liberty and Legalism.* The chapter is about eating in the context of being a "cultured Christian." Brett shares the story of a memorable Shabbat meal experienced with a group of twenty-something Messianic Jews in Los Angeles, describing the dinner as a "rich, sacred, long meal of prayers, songs, Scripture reading, laughing, and plenty of *'L'chaim!'* a toast that is a Jewish salutation meaning, 'To life!'"

Inspired by the culinary creativity of his friends, McCracken writes, "They remind me that food—the most quotidian and seemingly meaningless of all cultural items we daily consume—can be a significant experience in our lives, beyond just giving us the calories we need to keep moving."[2] McCracken inspires me to ponder how I can make our Sabbath meals convivial as well as sacred.

When my Aunt Paula and Uncle Jim visit from Oklahoma on Thanksgiving, we sit around our dining room table with chairs pushed back, lingering longer than usual to let the stuffing settle. Bantering back and forth, we share stories and laugh until our stomach muscles ache. We hold up gold-rimmed stem glasses—heirlooms from my grandparents—and toast with our own unique L'chaim! thanking God for his loving care and faithfulness. When the kids were little, they participated in making the meal celebratory by creating special place cards, hiding surprise questions beneath china plates, and making napkin holders from construction paper. Cloth napkins, polished silverware, candles, and gold chargers are on the table along with whatever I find on a nature scavenger hunt. A clipped branch of beauty berry and colored leaves decorate the table with hints of autumn. A few undetected tiny insects on cuttings incite more playful banter once they are spotted scurrying around the gravy boat.

I spend time thinking about how to make a holiday meal special and include my family members in the process. But what about making our Sabbath meal different? Can we toast L'chaim! every week? I think it's possible, so I quiz the Sabbath Society with questions and invite input. Natalie writes back, identifying the heart of celebration in one simple sentence: "Our Sabbath meals are about ease and togetherness."

Natalie chooses Sunday as her time to Sabbath and explains that often, after her family returns home from church, they eat a simple lunch together—fruit, veggies, sandwiches grilled with a variety of cheeses and meat—and each person creates his or her own plate. At the table, they connect about ideas from the sermon or things that have come up during the week. Natalie describes their Sabbath as a good time:

Sometimes I put together an easy fruit crisp in the afternoon or suggest that the girls and I make a pie for fun. Last time I did that, my husband discovered that none of the children had ever bobbed for apples, and I ended up making my pie alone while they bobbed for apples as though their lives depended on it. Every time I bring out a Sunday afternoon dessert, particularly if it is caramel apple pie, they respond as though they have received cool water in a parched desert. Our evenings usually involve games or a movie and a long-standing tradition of apples, cheese, and popcorn. It's the tradition that sustains.

After Moses led the Israelites out of Egypt, he used words to create imagery of abundance, blessing, and fruitfulness when he was speaking of God fulfilling his promise. He appealed to their felt needs with sensory overload, using words that describe—wait for it—food.

For the Lord your God is bringing you into a good land of flowing streams and pools of water, with fountains and springs that gush out in the valleys and hills. It is a land of wheat and barley; of grapevines, fig trees, and pomegranates; of olive oil and honey. It is a land where food is plentiful and nothing is lacking.

Deuteronomy 8:6–9 NLT

Being drawn to cook in preparation for rest is now a revelation instead of an oddity. When we are in seasons of life that don't make sense, when God seems to have turned around and walked down the street, our heart longs for a glimmer of the Promised Land. And cooking is one small step toward eternity. We touch, smell, taste, hear, and see heaven in small daily increments. In olive oil and garlic simmering in the skillet, in honey dripping off fresh bread, a cool drink of water on a hot day—these are all reminders of God's faithful presence with us. He keeps his promises.

Moses created hope by painting a picture with words that ignite our senses, and he also warns us that the way to live a long and prosperous life is about "[staying] on the path that the Lord your God has commanded you to follow" (Deuteronomy 5:33 NLT). He tells the Israelites to fear the Lord and love him with all of their heart, soul, and strength (6:5). And not to forget, in the midst of God's blessings, the care he provided in the wilderness. When our refrigerator is stocked with wants, every room bulges with possessions, and when lack is a distant memory, Moses warns us to be careful. "Beware that in your plenty you do not forget the Lord your God and disobey his commands, regulations, and decrees" (8:11–12 NLT).

Sabbath in the spirit of ease and togetherness cultivates a period of rest that is hospitable. The details really do matter. Making pies, eating popcorn, bobbing for apples, cloth napkins and china or paper plates, opening a bottle of bubbly or a can of Coke, looking people in the eyes and listening without the distraction of your cell phone—whatever makes the day feel special to you, makes it feel special to God. On Sabbath, what matters most is that the details are different than the other six days of the week. We think about how we can bless others by being fully present and we cultivate community with meaningful acts of joy.

Times set aside for rest can often be like a bowlful of lettuce, bland and tasteless, because I've been too busy to put much thought into it. Choices about how I celebrate are limited when I don't plan ahead. But when I prepare, Sabbath is loaded with beautiful color, texture, and saturated with the oil of gladness. And I'm full and contented when my time to rest is over. Like a good meal shared with a friend, I don't want the time to end, and I can't wait until the next time we meet together.

While we wait through the bureaucratic process of applying for visas, Murielle finishes the first semester of university, and Harrison misses the first three months of his sophomore year in high school. Our house is on the market with few showings, due to a downturn in the market. Random checks in various amounts appear in the mailbox from the most unlikely places, like manna, miraculous and sustaining. But Christmas is fast approaching. The family tree that stood in our living room for over a decade of Christmases was donated to Habitat for Humanity. Ornaments are packed and marked with *England* on the boxes. The hardest part? We can't afford to buy gifts for our kids, or anyone one else for that matter.

> For as long, then, as that promise of resting in him pulls us on to God's goal for us, we need to be careful that we're not disqualified. We received the same promises as those people in the wilderness, but the promises didn't do them a bit of good because they didn't receive the promises with faith. If we believe, though, we'll experience that state of resting. But not if we don't have faith.
>
> Hebrews 4:1–4 MSG

Will you believe? It's the question God asks of us in the wilderness.

Vacillating between exhaustion and angst, we learn that the date for moving to England is pushed back until the beginning of 2015. Praying through another setback, H and I sense this is a sabbatical God is providing for our family. Sabbatical? *Really?* In the same way Sarah laughs to herself when she overhears the Lord say she will have a child by the time he visits a year later, a sabbatical is not exactly what we wanted to hear. Sarah's words echo, "After I am worn out and my lord is old, will I now have this pleasure?" (Genesis 18:12).

H and I are doers. Tell us what to do and we'll make it happen. But do nothing? That is much harder. But God wasn't laughing with us. "Is anything too hard for the Lord?" (18:14).

When it comes to rest, we can pit our circumstances against God's promises and laugh about the disparity. "There remains, then, a Sabbath-rest for the people of God; for anyone who enters God's rest also rests from their works, just as God did from his" (Hebrews 4:9–10). We can translate his words into wishful thinking, think a rhythm of rest is not really possible, or assess wrongly based on our situation. And just like Sarah, he asks us why we are laughing. So we approach a sabbatical sober-minded.

Again, we sense God is asking, "What do you want me to do for you?" and determine fear will not influence our answer. We want to be with family and friends in Phoenix. We want to go home to the people who know us best. We want to remember that we belong. So we trust him to make a way for us to get there. And he does.

Instead of Geri coming to visit us on the Atlantic, we are visiting her in the desert. Over the hills of the south, through the plains of the mid-states, and serpentining under the painted skies of the southwest, we log miles on the odometer. Five days pushing pavement west, we visit friends and relatives for short periods of rest, and pull into the driveway of Geri's house in Phoenix. And exhale deeply. Respite among longtime friends and family during the last few weeks of Advent feels like the beginning of springtime, buds opening on barren branches, a small seed sprouting in what we began to assume were infertile plans for getting us to London.

Deep down in our marrow, we know the ruthless grace of what it means to wait for Christ to come. Micha Boyett says, "We all must learn how to hold great pleasure and great sorrow, always at the same time. What is joyful almost always carries a seed of sadness with it,"[3] and I agree. We carry the seeds of joy and sadness in our pockets as we break bread, feast, and heal in community, expectant while hesitant to fully hope.

On Christmas morning, I lament about the lack of gifts under the tree for everyone. "I don't do guilt," Geri reminds me.

New Year's Eve brings a surprise—a phone call from our Realtor with much anticipated news: an offer on the sale of our house. It seems as if God is beginning to stretch the bow back in preparation to set us free to soar. Or are we speculating once again?

We crack open a bottle of bubbly and celebrate L'chaim! by dipping squares of brown bread pierced on the ends of long forks into creamy cheddar fondue. And we wait for the new to begin.

Chapter Twelve

Wings of Rescue

What comes into our minds when we think about God is really the most important thing about us.

A.W. Tozer, *The Knowledge of the Holy*

Early on a Wednesday, I run from my office into the bedroom exclaiming, "I told you so!" Only to find H in bed, talking on the phone in a somber tone: "Uh-huh" and "No, I understand."

Propping myself up against pillows next to him, I pull the duvet up to my waist and listen to the end of the conversation, drawing shallow breaths. H tells me our Realtor has had trouble sleeping, praying all night and dreading the delivery of our good news turning bad. The buyers have changed their minds on the purchase of our house for reasons that elude all the players involved in the contract.

I can assume the good news received on New Year's Eve about our house selling was ultimately an act of meanness, a test of faith I am certain to fail with an indignant knee-jerk emotional reaction. Or, I can trust God and believe he works all things together for my good, even in the midst of disappointment and what many assumed was an answer to prayer.

I chose the first, then I changed my mind. The biggest hurdle we face as followers of Jesus is resisting assumptions about the way God feels about us based on circumstances. The ways of God cannot be figured out, explained, or reasoned into some kind of Hallmark understanding. When I want explanation for pain or suffering, I discount the mystery. Finding resolution becomes about me, not God's purposes.

His love for us is not determined by or relative to the outcomes of any problems or difficulties. Perhaps that is why he healed on the Sabbath,[1] for the way it dispelled any rumors. Jesus is determined not to allow you to place him in a tidy little box.

The phone call feels like a punch in the gut, but I notice something surprising as I listen to H explain the details. Trust is building a stronger faith muscle each time we circle around an issue bringing undesirable news. Each encounter holds the opportunity for faith to deepen and the healing of wounds to take place. And each time an incident triggers doubt, we bounce back more quickly to health and a wholehearted stance.

The next day, during a quiet time of reading the Scriptures, I am stopped by the word *arrow* in Psalm 18. God is highlighting another word in the same way he did the word *writ*. I research the meaning of *arrow* in Scripture, but I'm not finding anything substantive—nothing new or revolutionary—until I read the passage in *The Message*. I'm a visual thinker and the imagery in the words of this translation stick much faster. What I conclude about the arrow when cited in Scripture is this: Arrows are often associated with God as a warrior in the midst of battle.

From his palace he hears my call; my cry brings me right into his presence—a private audience! Earth wobbles and lurches; huge mountains shake like leaves, quake like aspen leaves because of his rage. His nostrils flare, bellowing smoke; his mouth spits fire. Tongues of fire dart in and out; he lowers the sky. He steps down;

under his feet an abyss opens up. He's riding a winged creature, swift on wind-wings. Now he's wrapped himself in a trench coat of black-cloud darkness. But his cloud-brightness bursts through, spraying hailstones and fireballs. Then God thundered out of heaven; the High God gave a great shout, spraying hailstones and fireballs. God shoots his arrows—pandemonium! . . . But me he caught—reached all the way from sky to sea; he pulled me out of that ocean of hate, that enemy chaos, the void in which I was drowning. They hit me when I was down, but God stuck by me. He stood me up on a wide-open field; I stood there saved—surprised to be loved!

Psalm 18:6–14, 16–19

As I close my eyes, the arrows I first glimpsed when looking out the window of the plane come flying back through my mind, breaking up thoughts with images of busy London streets crowded with people. The point barely grazes the faces of several who are oblivious to the danger. The arrow flies continuously around the city at breakneck speed without landing on a specific target.

When I walk back into the bedroom, H shudders upon my entrance. He isn't normally skittish, so the reaction stops me in my tracks. I learn he is deep in thought, preparing prayerfully for an imminent Skype chat with the two leaders in London, people responsible for the jobs allowing us to live there on visas. His eyes tell me he is weary from waiting, wanting to be strong, but the loss of the sale on the house makes him feel vulnerable. Three steps forward and two steps back, when we assumed we were already on the backside of the mountain we've been climbing for months.

In the headline news from the television in the bedroom, two U.S. climbers are being interviewed after they conquer the face of El Capitan in Yosemite National Park. I can't help but see their climb as a metaphor for our waiting season. Their fingers are cracked with fissures, raw and bleeding. During the climb they sleep on flat pieces of rock under tents, harnessed with ropes to prevent a deadly fall. After two weeks, they are weary and admit their resolve waned under the harsh conditions, yet they reached the summit of the three-thousand-foot rock. Kevin Jorgeson, thirty, and Tommy Caldwell, thirty-six, make history as the first climbers to do so without aids.[2] Though our situations are completely different, I see a parallel in the race of endurance. I want to give up when things get too hard and slide down the rope to familiar safety. But in my heart, I know the finish line is just a few days off. I must persevere and trust in Jesus for rescue.

All of us face the same dilemma every week with Sabbath. Pressures of life become weighty and unmanageable; we want to slide back into work or doing something that brings comfort. When tiredness breaks our resolve, we are tempted to give up rest instead of trusting in what God has for us in Sabbath.

H wraps his arms around me after watching the news footage and leans back to look into my eyes for consolation. I tell him I've been praying and explain how God brought back the arrows.

"Me too," he says. "I had that same impression in my prayers this morning." He reminds me that *we* are the arrows God is shooting and how it is impossible to control the direction an arrow takes once it launches from the bow: all you can do is wait, ride it out, and see where it lands when it comes out of the shadows. God is speaking through another metaphor, and although the metaphors aren't changing anything in particular for us, the echo of the arrow in morning prayers provides comfort and confirmation that he is near and working out the details.

Two hours later, H is sitting in the family room, on his call, and I am pacing the floor in the next room, praying silently while reciting the character of God revealed in the Psalms. Nervous energy pulses through my body. I message my friend Dea, who intercedes for us regularly: "Listening in. Feeling sick to my stomach, I'm so nervous."

Within seconds, she writes back, "I reminded God of his character and our assurance of commitment to his will on the earth as it is in heaven. I am so with you in my heart. I know you have to be teetering, but there are mighty wings to catch you."

And there it is: through the practice of adoration, God's presence is revealed in her words back to me—*mighty wings to catch you,* words expressing similar imagery from Psalm 18. Dea could've used any words when she responded, but God knew those particular words would hold special meaning for me, fresh with revelation.

H finishes his call with prayer, and when he walks into the room he is smiling, looking relieved and happy. He has met the final requirements in the process for sponsorship that allow us to receive visas to live in England. The arrow is pulled taut on the bow, ready to launch once the paperwork is finished.

More waiting.

The next day, midafternoon, I receive a call from my friend Sue. She has heard the news about the sale of our house going bust and wants to tell me she is sorry and praying for us while we wait. I tell her I'm tired, on the tattered end of the frayed knot of patience. Tears stop me mid-sentence.

"You have been through so much; God is with you," she assures. "Jesus *is* Sabbath. And Sabbath is finding rest in him."

It's a warm, balmy day in January. I take a walk for solace under a canopy of sunshine. I long to be less of a feeler, to process this season more rationally and with less emotion. I don't want to hurt anyone with words spewing out of my mouth in reaction. I don't trust myself when I'm anxious. But if I stuff emotions, thoughts travel to a dark place and I have trouble seeing my way out.

> "For my thoughts are not your thoughts, neither are your ways my ways," declares the Lord. "As the heavens are higher than the earth, so are my ways higher than your ways and my thoughts than your thoughts."
>
> Isaiah 55:8–9

How can I turn off my mind? How can I enjoy life without assigning meaning to everything? How can I numb my emotions and still feel God's presence with me, without compromising our relationship? These questions become the basis of my next letter to the Sabbath Society. I call it The Practice of Not Thinking.

I tell them about the sale of our house falling through and admit my emotions are on high alert and coping mechanisms faulty. Whenever well-laid plans are interrupted by disappointment, peace abruptly halts. I confess the practical steps we make in preparation for making Sabbath a rich experience may actually be the easiest part. We can have all the components in place—clean house, errand list checked, stocked refrigerator, food simmering for the weekend—all while the mind is in a constant state of restlessness, working tirelessly and unfocused. Ironically, I give them a list of things *to do* to achieve a mind at rest. And if Jesus *is* Sabbath, then the way to achieve peace isn't about doing more but resting in him. If Jesus is Sabbath and we are made in his image, then we carry the spirit of Sabbath within us that makes resting body, mind, and soul possible.

Solomon loved the Lord, it says in the book of 1 Kings. He walked in the statutes of David his father and he sacrificed and made offerings in high places. Solomon offered a thousand burnt offerings on an altar, showing his great love for the Lord, but it wasn't until he was sleeping that God appeared to him. While at rest, God broke through a dream and spoke with a request: "Ask for whatever you want me to give you" (1 Kings 3:5).

And there it is again—the same question he asked of me when I was wrestling to find peace at the cottage in Canada. "What do you want me to do for you?" It's the question we hear him ask when we are at the end of our striving. Solomon's answer pleased God and revealed he was attentive and ready:

> Here's what I want: Give me a God-listening heart so I can lead your people well, discerning the difference between good and evil. For who on their own is capable of leading your glorious people?
>
> 1 Kings 3:9 MSG

I am a student of Sabbath, with a listening heart as a result, and like Solomon, I am attempting to discern between good and evil and lead people to find rest—listening to the words God is highlighting in the Scriptures, identifying his voice echoing through the wisdom of the trusted, listening to the past, and listening on behalf of others. That morning I woke up at the lake with the word *writ* trailing through my sleepy thoughts was preparation for staying awake, for harnessing the epistles he is writing about our future. Henri Nouwen writes,

A life lived in expectation is like a life in which we have received a letter, a letter which makes him whom we have missed so much return even earlier than we could imagine. Expectation brings joy to the center of our sadness and the loved one to the heart of our longings.[3]

Almost two years later, weary of striving as I wait, I learn that peace comes not when God gives what I seek, but when I believe he will come *because he loves me.* God waited for thousands of years before he sent his only Son.

On Sunday morning, we sleep in past eight and skip church. We cannot bear the questions asked of us repeatedly about moving to London when all we have are vague answers. A lack of concrete plans after leaving a good job with broad influence is an exercise in relinquishing reputation. Sometimes letting go is painful, and today we choose not to suffer.

I pick up Preston Yancey's *Tables in the Wilderness* lying in a book bag of freebies I had received, drawn to crack it open before all the equally good options. After reading the first chapter, understanding comes. The book happens to be about a season of spiritual wilderness—a struggle with trust during a period of God's silence. When I reach the last paragraph in the first chapter, it's as if God is talking directly to me. The words I'm reading go suddenly blurry.

Stop doing. Stop striving. Stop. You're in the middle place. You're on the plateau. Here is the table before you. This is the wilderness. You have arrived somewhere. God has brought you to somewhere.

He said it would be about trust, and you see, it is. You're in this somewhere space, this wilderness space. Now go and have a look around.[4]

Chills prickle the hairs on my arms and legs. My eyes spill over with tears, soaking my pajama top. And suddenly I realize today is Sabbath.

The book of Revelation describes continual upheaval and a lack of rest as the ultimate separation from God:

> He will be tormented with fire and sulfur in the presence of the holy angels and in the presence of the Lamb. And the smoke of their torment goes up forever and ever, and they have no rest, day or night.
>
> 14:10–11 esv

Striving and a lack of rest in body, soul, and mind ultimately results in a tormented life. But God provides rescue in the next verse: "Here is a call for the endurance of the saints, those who keep the commandments of God and their faith in Jesus" (14:12 esv).

How do we endure? How do we quiet our mind? How do we achieve peace in the midst of upheavals in life? We keep the commandments of God, and the result is a wholehearted life. It seems so simple, but his precepts really are trustworthy. I've searched the Word as a lamp lighting the unknowns in the dark leg of this journey. I've fallen asleep pleading heaven, and yet all the mental activity running fiercely toward resolution has hindered what God intended. He longed for me to quietly wait for him to come in Sabbath. I've wearied myself with mental work while doubting the purpose of the truth scribed in the fourth commandment.

Andrew Murray writes,

> He stirs up your nest. He disappoints your hopes. He brings down your confidence. He makes you fear and tremble, as all your strength fails, and you feel utterly weary and helpless. And all the while He is spreading His strong wings for you to rest your weakness on,

and offering His everlasting Creator-strength to work in you. And all He asks is that you sink down in your weariness and wait on Him; and allow Him in His Jehovah-strength to carry you as you ride upon the wings of His Omnipotence.[5]

♦ ♦ ♦

I read in the newspaper how Han Jin Sook, a South Korean mother, speaks about the challenges facing her eighteen-year-old son. Once a model student at the top of his class, addiction is now threatening to ruin his life. He has dropped out of school, become uncharacteristically aggressive, stressed, and withdrawn. His addiction, however, is not to drugs or alcohol but technology. Ten hours a day his mind is swirling with information. He lives, works, and plays with his mind in constant hypervigilance. In desperation, his mother sends him to a digital-detox boot camp.[6] And don't we all need to detox our soul, mind, and body from busyness? Sabbath is a weekly boot camp for rescuing a tormented life.

"What deadens us most to God's presence within us, I think, is the inner dialogue that we are continuously engaged in with ourselves, the endless chatter of human thought," Frederick Buechner's words echo.[7] So I revisit Psalm 111:7, the verse that jolted my life awake: *"All his precepts are trustworthy."*

Yes! I see it now as I look back through the porthole of waiting. God's precepts express his love and faithfulness as much as the works of his hands. His love has been the motivation for our waiting season all along. I just couldn't detect his presence through the anxiety and uncertainty. "The precepts of the Lord are right, rejoicing the heart; the commandment of the Lord is pure, enlightening the eyes" (Psalm 19:8 ESV).

This psalm is a song of celebration, rejoicing in all the great things God has done. He calls us to be his own, cared for and protected. And all he asks of us in return is that we believe him in the fear of the Lord. He gives us dominion over the earth and all he has made is good. And then, before he chisels the words of the Ten Commandments, he makes a covenant with us:

Before all your people I will do marvels, such as have not been created in all the earth or in any nation. And all the people among whom you are shall see the work of the Lord, for it is an awesome thing that I will do with you.

Exodus 34:10 ESV

We want to know that our waiting is not in vain, and he promises it won't be. The result of our waiting will be an awesome thing he will do for us when we trust him. I wait for the fulfillment of things to come to pass, when Jesus longs for me to wait for him to come. I can do the first, but only he can do the last. When I approach the fourth commandment as a suggestion, I am not responding in the fear of the Lord. Relinquishment of outcomes precedes the miracle he wants to do in and through us. "He remembers his covenant forever" (Psalm 105:8).

Just as God remembers, so should we. In the beginning, he remembers Noah, and then he remembers us with a rainbow (Genesis 8–9). He remembers his covenant forever, the word that he commanded, for a thousand generations, and the covenant that he made with Abraham (Psalm 105:8–11). Sabbath is a holy writ—his love letter to us once a week. When we believe him by obeying the commandment of Sabbath, his face shines upon us the same way it did on Moses. And everyone notices the brightness.

He is asking you to remember the Sabbath. Will you?

❦ ❦ ❦

The second contract on the house sticks. We sell furniture and give away possessions like it's Christmas around the maple tree in the front yard. H packs Murielle's bedroom furniture, our antiques and keepsakes—all in a storage unit, like piecing together a giant puzzle. A friend in Tennessee buys our van, sight unseen, after I mention needing to sell it in a status update on Facebook. H orders a crate, delivered to our driveway, and packs it with household goods to be loaded on a ship sailing for England. Christmas dishes are packed alongside the delicate blue glass Shabbat candlesticks, protected by mounds of paper.

We accept a friend's offer of a week at his hotel on the Atlantic, in Myrtle Beach, to help with easing our transition. After waiting for months, we're caught up in a whirlwind of activity (just like God told me it would happen on the plane from Dallas).

And then the *better than we could have imagined* comes true. A house in London suddenly becomes available to us: newer, updated, with a garage and garden, in a quiet part of the city where shop owners and neighbors are on a first-name basis. Had we arrived earlier, it wouldn't have been an option due to tenants with leases. It's located in our favorite part of London—we never considered living in one of the most expensive neighborhoods a reality. And then God kisses me on the cheek with this little revelation: the house is located near a park called Brookgreen. The serendipity and redemption? It's better than we could have imagined! God cares about the details, because in the details, he reveals the depth of his love for us.

The details are why we were waiting to move to England. The details are why he wants us to wait for him in Sabbath.

On our last night as residents of South Carolina, H drives us in a borrowed truck from a restaurant back to the hotel. He and Harrison complain of muscle soreness after loading final boxes from the house into the truck, and off into the storage unit—eight times—like drawing over the same circle until the paper is thin and threatening to rip apart. As we pull into a parking space and unclasp our seat belts, the vibration of the phone in my purse syncopates our movement toward the hotel. When I look at the screen, I realize it's my literary agent. He is calling to tell me he has concrete offers on my book proposal. Our move and the book are intertwined (just like God promised on that same Dallas flight).

The next morning, an early alarm opens my sleepy eyes to the sun rising orange over an endless stretch of placid ocean, gulls floating quietly. A clutch of college girls laugh while walking a stretch of beach punctuated with singles and pairs jogging and walking pets on leashes. From the high-rise hotel, I stare over the vastness of sky meeting water and wonder over what God is planning for us beyond the horizon, on the shores of England. I am bone-tired, but I feel like the luckiest girl on the beach, because I am flying to London to stay for more than just a few weeks. We pack suitcases, check consignment accounts for funds from the sale of our furniture, and run a few last-minute errands for items we won't find in England. Keys to the front door are now mementos.

We arrive at the airport, pulling our overnight bags, filled with computers and books. I find a quiet place to sit on a deserted row of white vinyl seats, overlooking a wall of windows before the empty tarmac. March is warming up at the beach, but I'm wearing boots and carrying a black trench coat in preparation for chilly temperatures in London. As I watch the sun set like a turning kaleidoscope, colors bleed blue into violet, then amber and pink.

Swift on wind-wings, reaching all the way from sky to sea, God launches us—his arrows—and we fly over the sun setting golden through the window. He comes. He rescues us from the darkness of a long waiting season. And the following day, I stand in London, saved—surprised to be loved so deeply.

> I heard a voice out of Heaven, "Write this: Blessed are those who die in the Master from now on; how blessed to die that way!"
>
> "Yes," says the Spirit, "and blessed rest from their hard, hard work. None of what they've done is wasted; God blesses them for it all in the end."
>
> Revelation 14:13 MSG

Practical Prompts
for Sabbath Pauses

Chapter 1: Baby Steps

1. Sabbath became a surprising answer to questions about belonging. Have you ever considered Sabbath as a way to cultivate a sense of belonging?

2. I admit that in the past I approached Sabbath as a suggestion or an elective instead of a commandment. How have your views about Sabbath been shaped in the past?

3. What emotion does the word *Sabbath* conjure up for you?

4. How do preconceived ideas about Sabbath block a rhythm of rest in your life?

5. How do you respond to things being left undone in order to rest? Is guilt a factor in choosing not to rest?

6. I describe similarities between Sabbath and Advent as a time pregnant with expectancy and longing. How does this change the way you envision Sabbath?

7. Preparation is one of the keys for a rich Sabbath experience. Share some of the practical ways you can prepare during the week in order to make rest a reality.

8. I explain that the idea of a discipline becomes a successful part of life when practiced in community. As you begin to take baby steps toward a weekly rhythm of Sabbath, is there someone you might ask to join you for accountability?

9. This week, meditate on the fourth commandment (Exodus 20:8). Read it in several Bible translations, and then note anything new or insightful about the words and their intended meanings.

Chapter 2: Questions and One-Word Answers

1. I have painted a picture of a busy, stress-filled life and the way a vacation is my recovery room. Do you think of times away as stress-inducing, an escape from life, a needed respite and/or a time of greater attentiveness to God's presence with you? Use two words to describe how your life feels at the moment. Examples: tired and weary, content and curious, anxious and lonely.

2. Explain how being disconnected from the mundane aspects of daily work life can be a reorientation toward what is most important. On a scale of 1 to 10, how would you rate your current life perspective? 1 = foggy and 10 = standing on a mountaintop with clear vistas before you.

3. How much time in your day/week do you dedicate to quiet, stillness, and reflection? How can you begin to reorient your days to make these disciplines a reality?

4. Have you ever thought about creating intentions for rest in the same way you are intentional about the other parts of your life? If not, write down some specific steps you can take toward making rest a rhythm of your life this week.

5. Turn those goals into specific prayer requests.

6. This week, take a walk in a new place or sit somewhere alone with your morning coffee or in a new spot during a lunch break. Take mental notes or write down the sounds and sights you might normally overlook when hurried on the inside. How does this exercise make you feel? Examples: rejuvenated, rushed, worried, peaceful, introspective.

Chapter 3: Prayers and Epistles

1. Have you ever thought about Sabbath as a weekly invitation for conversation with the Creator, not only for you but for others? Does this idea change your perspective about how you approach a day of rest?

2. "Sabbath-keeping provides good practice in discernment." Is this a new concept? Has this been your experience?

3. Tell about a time when you risked boldly to share with someone encouragement, Scripture, or warning that came from a time of prayer. Or perhaps a prayer time resulted in personal application. Either way, how did that time of listening make a difference for you or someone else?

4. Noticing is a learned art. This week, practice paying attention to the ways God is afoot in your everyday life like a lab technician looking through a microscope. Write down the petals you notice in the bouquet or in essence, the details of divine presence. Take note of any patterns.

5. There are three ways to respond to the leading of the Holy Spirit: (1) Ask for wise counsel from the spiritually mature, (2) wait for confirmation, or (3) accept an answer that isn't preferred but resonates with truth. Think of a scenario in your past when you've either been the recipient or applied these principles with someone.

6. Are there more ways you've experienced being mentored by the Holy Spirit when it comes to applying pieces of prayerful discernment? If so, share them.

7. Practice listening prayer this week and write down what comes to your mind. Words, pictures, sentences—nothing is random or insignificant. Stay alert to an answer in the days ahead.

Chapter 4: Dispelling Myths

1. I shared that sometimes I am hesitant to talk about Sabbath in the same way I am sensitive about sharing my faith with new acquaintances. Have you experienced this situation?

2. I define the difference between *being* the church versus *doing* church. Have you ever thought about Sabbath as being the church instead of doing church? How does this juxtaposition change your perspective about Sabbath?

3. Does the fear of legalism keep you from making Sabbath a weekly rhythm? Or can you relate with my experience of ignorance about the fourth commandment?

4. If your view of Sabbath was shaped by legalism, dispel some of those myths by sharing them with someone you trust. Pray that God will begin to shape a new understanding about Sabbath in a way that is personally life-giving for you.

5. This week, write down some of the false messages you've heard about Sabbath and surrender them to Jesus. Meditate on Matthew 11:28–30; journal how God is replacing misguided perspectives with truth.

6. How can Sabbath be a way of evangelism to those with whom you relate and influence? If we are called to be separated from the world and different from the norms society dictates, think about how Sabbath communicates that difference to people who are looking for hope.

Chapter 5: From How to Who

1. Can you identify with the questions asked in this chapter as an indicator you are overdue for rest?

2. How do you struggle with the practical aspects of making Sabbath a reality?

3. Have you thought about making time for rest on a day other than Sunday? What are some practical baby steps you can take to make a window of rest a reality?

4. Take time this week to do something just for you. Visit somewhere new, walk another path, meet a friend for a chat—something that isn't about obtaining a preferred outcome. Share what you learn from the experience.

5. What are some small ways you can begin to trust God with your time this week? Share them with an accountability partner.

Chapter 6: Stop or Be Forced to Stop

1. How do you usually respond to interruptions?

2. Can you see interruptions as "arm chair altars"? As small windows of time that God may be orchestrating in order to cultivate relationship with you?

3. Is the concept of being broken in the right and wrong places a new one for you? Identify the way brokenness affects our ability to rest.

4. Have you ever considered natural disaster, illness, or trauma a kind of forced Sabbath? How does this affect the way you respond to interruptions?

5. I share about the ways Sabbath and optimum health are curiously linked. Explain a time in your life when rest has been a catalyst for reviving your soul and body. Or explain the way you have witnessed this in someone else.

6. When you don't have a snowstorm or hurricane as an excuse to rest, how do you create space and order time for Sabbath?

Chapter 7: Watch for the Arrows

1. Remember a time when you were surprised by the way God answered a prayer. Did the answer seem unusual, ridiculous, or too silly to tell someone about? How could he be answering your prayers the same way now?
2. Read the story of Noah in Genesis 5:32–10:1. What made Noah distinctive? What are the qualities Noah possessed that made him a desirable candidate to be used by God in such a big way?
3. What is the ark God is asking you to build for him? That thing only you can do because of the qualities that make you distinctive? How can intentional Sabbath rhythms help you achieve your calling and purpose?
4. I mention the way God selects leaders who teach us how to live. Can you identify some of those leaders in your life? How have they shaped you, both positively and negatively, for your ultimate good and God's purposes in your life?
5. If God is leaving arrows to guide us in the details of life, what might those arrows be for you currently? Begin journaling some of the arrows you notice God highlighting in your daily life.
6. In order to be compassionate toward the needs of those around us, we must first allow self-compassion. When was the last time you were compassionate toward yourself? What are some practical ways you can practice self-compassion this week?
7. I mention that we can rest fully when we believe we are worthy of rest. Ask God to show what worthiness looks like from his

perspective. Take one step toward expressing your worthiness as part of Sabbath-keeping this week.

Chapter 8: Extravagant Wastefulness

1. Do you tend to value time according to utility? If so, how can you begin to change the way you think about "wasting time" in order to rest?
2. Knowing that daydreaming and idleness are indispensable for optimal brain function, does this change your definition of how you spend time?
3. Have you ever associated pausing and silence as an act of bravery? Think of a time in your life when silence made a positive impact for you and upon others.
4. What are some of the practical ways you can begin to include pausing or solitude during the week?
5. Is play a natural part of your life? Or do you associate play with foreboding joy? Include play somewhere in your week and write down how playing made you feel inside.
6. Sit somewhere quiet, alone, for ten minutes. Write down all the things you hear, smell, and see in that small window. Share your list with someone. What you miss in busyness might astound you.

Chapter 9: Uncertainty: Rest and Love Are Connected

1. Rest and love are connected. Identify places in your life where hustle may be communicating a subversive message that you are unlovable.
2. We are more capable of resting when we feel loved. Meditate on the ways you have felt loved recently. How does the

connection between love and rest apply to your current life situation?

3. How does the need for certainty sabotage your weekly rhythm of rest?

4. If you do less, do you feel you are somehow less?

5. Answer this question: If I do more, I feel more _____ (fill in the blank).

6. How can *more* be a counterfeit for love?

7. I discovered the need for certainty was an idol keeping me from peace. How has the fear of uncertainty blocked you from trusting God?

8. Random coincidences can often provide beacons of hope—smells attached to memories, conversations over dinner and during commutes, reading a story or Bible verse that becomes an answer for a lingering curiosity. Begin to pay attention to the world around you and take note of how God may be speaking to you differently.

Chapter 10: Preparation Is Everything

1. Preparation is everything when it comes to successful Sabbath-keeping. What are a few practical things you can do this week to prepare for a day of rest?

2. Do you believe God uses limits to fulfill his purposes? How can you begin to see the narrowing of your time as God's highest intention for you this week?

3. Read Philippians 2:5–11. If Jesus limited himself, how does the concealment of his gifts inform your life?

4. If God is resetting your boundaries, how do you embrace and honor limits with your time?

5. What does living well look like for you in this season of your life?

6. "Idealism is the thief of Sabbath." Think of how this statement applies to your situation. Share your thoughts in a journal or talk about it with someone.

7. This week, begin paying attention to interruptions on Sabbath. Practice listening prayer by asking God to help you distinguish providential interruptions from distractions.

Chapter 11: L'Chaim! To Life!

1. What is your ruminating practice of choice? If you don't have one, explore ways you can begin to implement one activity that allows your mind to settle in preparation for Sabbath (e.g., coloring in an adult coloring book, gardening, hiking, cooking, journaling).

2. What are some of the practical ways you can make Sabbath feel different and celebratory this week? Try something new that makes the day feel different. Use cloth napkins, light new candles, sip something special, or visit a friend.

3. Think back to some of your most memorable meals and list some of the components that made it stand out to you. How can you begin to toast L'chaim! weekly and not just on special occasions?

4. Invite friends to join you for a Sabbath meal.

5. I shared about the incremental changes I make in preparing for Sabbath. On the day after you make the choice to Sabbath, start a list of what you need to accomplish in order to make rest a reality. Ask someone to hold you accountable.

6. Ask for help with one thing on your list.

7. Is doing nothing hard for you? If so, explain.

Chapter 12: Wings of Rescue

1. I describe struggling with resting my mind as the hardest part of Sabbath-keeping. Is this something you have experienced?

2. Quiet your mind by mediating on Matthew 11:28–30 (preferably in *The Message* version), contemplating one sentence at a time in your heart. As you slowly ponder each word, allow the truth to absorb all the things unsettling your spirit.

3. God cares about the details. How does this truth inform times of waiting?

4. Is it tempting for you to "slide back down the mountain" when Sabbath becomes hard due to circumstances? Recount the ways God has provided for you in the past when you've pushed past resistance.

5. I describe Sabbath as a day to wait for Jesus to come. How does this change the way you view Sabbath now?

6. "Striving and a lack of rest in body, soul, and mind ultimately results in a tormented life." How has this been illustrated for you in the past? Or currently?

7. Jesus is Sabbath. How does this truth change the way you will approach finding a rhythm of rest?

Acknowledgments

This book has my name on the spine, but perhaps it should also credit the Sabbath Society. Without contributions from the people who are endeavoring weekly to make Sabbath a priority, each chapter would be less than what God intended. Though these pages contain a small fraction of the letters exchanged between me and individuals, I am indebted to the brave souls who risked an unusual vulnerability by writing to me about personal trials and intimate prayer requests. I'm honored that you said "I'm all in" when it comes to making rest a rhythm of life. Thank you for trusting me with your stories, prayers, and successes.

As with most great achievements in life, more has been birthed into existence by prayer than anything else we can possibly imagine. Thank you to a team of prayer warriors who asked, ushered in, and believed in the power of the Holy Spirit on my behalf.

For three spiritual midwives who coached me through the labor and delivery process of writing my first book—Lynn Morrissey, Dea Moore, and Mary Gemmill—this book is your baby, too. Lynn, for introducing me to Chip MacGregor, mentoring me in the curious ways of the writing life, and teaching the value of being a fan of someone's gifts. Dea, for holding out a life raft for us in a million different ways; you have taught this only child what it means to have a sister. Mary, for being a safe place and for practicing the art of listening prayer on my behalf. Your prophetic gift continues to be a source of joy and divine direction.

Multitasking isn't one of my strengths, but distraction and I are best buddies. I am indebted to Fred and Joyce McCune and Michael and Avril Denton, who loaned weeks of time away in their beautiful homes for quiet writing retreats. Your generosity is an extravagant blessing, and Emerald Isle in North Carolina and Chipping Camden in the United Kingdom will always be fond Sabbath destinations.

For every single blog reader at RedemptionsBeauty.com who commented, shared, emailed, and loved me with notes—thank you from the bottom of my heart. Your support and encouragement made this book possible.

I never would have risked leaving a job to pursue writing from passion without Terry Walling, my leadership coach. Thank you for challenging me with your awesome questions. I am living a dream because of your influence.

For faithful friends who held my hand during each unknown step of the writing journey into publishing: Jennifer Dukes Lee, Deidra Riggs, Michelle DeRusha, Kris Camealy, Kristin Schell, Laura Boggess, Heather Kopp, Misha Thompson, Emily Wierenga, Carey Bailey, and Elizabeth Marshall. You make my writing life so much richer. Thank you for your belief in me.

For Mark Buchanan, one of my mentors in the faith through words penned in his books. A dream on my bucket list came true when you said yes to endorsing my work and writing the Foreword. Thank you for paying it forward.

For Margaret Feinberg, the way you open doors, sacrifice time, and lavishly give away experience—your friendship and wisdom are a treasure.

My lovely English girlfriends who cheered me on, read my manuscript, gave me the very best (loving) constructive criticism, opened doors with influencers, and then actually applied the content with alacrity. Helen Cockram, Susanna Wright, and Lucinda Van Der Hart, you are God's gifts for such a time as this. Thank you!

For the friend I call whenever I am in the deepest depths, on the highest mountaintops, or whenever I have a new book I want to share with someone: LuAnn Nystrom, I am a writer because of your belief in God's good gifts stirred up within me.

For the first email I received in my inbox from Chip MacGregor, asking if I ever thought about becoming an author. You helped to make me one, and I am grateful you are in my corner.

Thank you, Jeff Braun, my editor at Bethany House Publishers. I'm indebted to you for believing in the vision of this book and taking a personal interest in it. Our phone conversation in the airport on the way to London will always be a treasured moment.

Murielle and Harrison, you remind me every day through the ways you respond to life that rhythms matter and rest isn't about *how* but *who*. I'm proud to be your mom. Thank you for supporting me through my technology learning curves and a brief addiction to blogging.

For my faithful H, who listens, loves, cheers, corrects, celebrates, and cries with me. Every day you teach me about the realities of grace, and I am richer for it. Thank you for sharing your mother, Geri—one of God's greatest gifts to me from our union.

Notes

Beginnings

1. Amy Langfield, "Unused Vacation Days at 40-Year High," CNBC, October 23, 2014, http://www.cnbc.com/2014/10/23/unused-vacation-days-at-40-year-high .html.

2. My definitions for routines and rhythms were inspired by Myquillyn Smith in her blog post for (in)courage, "Let the Rhythm Move You," August 27, 2014, http://www.incourage.me/2014/08/let-the-rhythm-move-you.html.

3. Exodus 20.

Chapter 1: Baby Steps

1. "Blessings and Instructions for Shabbat Candles," Chabad.org, http://www .chabad.org/library/article_cdo/aid/87131/jewish/Shabbat-Candles-Instructions .htm.

2. Brené Brown, *Daring Greatly* (New York: Gotham Books, 2012), Kindle edition, Loc. 2821.

3. Margaret Feinberg, *Wonderstruck* (Brentwood, TN: Worthy Publishing, 2012), 66.

4. This section on Advent inspired by Kimberlee Conway Ireton, *The Circle of Seasons: Meeting God in the Church Year* (Downers Grove, IL: InterVarsity Press, 2008), 17–24.

Chapter 2: Questions and One-Word Answers

1. Pat Conroy, *My Reading Life* (New York: Doubleday, 2010), 49.

2. Madeline L'Engle, *Walking on Water* (New York: North Point Press, 1980), 98.

3. Mark 10:36; 10:51.

4. Mark Batterson, *The Circle Maker* (Grand Rapids, MI: Zondervan, 2011), 23.

Chapter 3: Prayers and Epistles

1. Oxford Dictionaries, http://www.oxforddictionaries.com/definition/english/precept.

2. Merriam-Webster, http://www.merriam-webster.com/dictionary/writ.

3. John J. Parsons, "Ten Commandments," Hebrew for Christians, http://www.hebrew4christians.com/Scripture/Torah/Ten_Cmds/ten_cmds.html.

4. *The Free Dictionary*, http://thefreedictionary.com/epistolary.

5. A.W. Tozer, *The Pursuit of God* (Camp Hill, PA: Christian Publications, 1982, 1993).

6. Frederick Buechner, *Listening to Your Life* (New York: HarperCollins, 1992).

7. This section informed by Lauren Winner in *Mudhouse Sabbath* (Brewster, MA: Paraclete Press, 2003), 8.

8. Tozer, *The Pursuit of God*, 59.

9. Acts 18:24–26.

10. Mark 8:22–26.

11. Mark 8:31–32.

Chapter 4: Dispelling Myths

1. Abraham Joshua Heschel, *The Sabbath* (New York: Farrar, Straus, and Giroux, 1951), 41.

Chapter 5: From How to Who

1. Steven Pressfield, *The War of Art* (New York: Black Irish Entertainment, 2002), Kindle edition, Loc. 220.

2. Information from *Urban Dictionary*, http://www.urbandictionary.com/define.php?term=resistance+is+futile.

3. Pressfield, *The War of Art*, Kindle edition, Loc. 49.

4. Ibid., Kindle edition, Loc. 236.

5. Julia Cameron, *The Right to Write* (New York: Putnam, 1998), 64–67.

6. Margaret Feinberg coined this phrase in her book *The Sacred Echo* (Grand Rapids, MI: Zondervan, 2012).

Chapter 6: Stop or Be Forced to Stop

1. Mark Buchanan, *Spiritual Rhythms* (Grand Rapids, MI: Zondervan, 2010), 281.

2. Alan E. Nelson, *Embracing Brokenness* (Colorado Springs, CO: NavPress, 2002), 70.

3. Ibid., 44.

4. Eugene Peterson, *The Jesus Way*, Kindle version, Loc. 1293.

5. Daniel A. Gross, "This Is Your Brain on Silence," *Nautilus,* August 21, 2014, http://nautil.us/issue/16/nothingness/this-is-your-brain-on-silence.

6. Ibid.

7. Ibid.

8. Wayne Muller, *Sabbath* (New York: Bantam Book, 1999), 25.

Chapter 7: Watch for the Arrows

1. "What Is ME/CFS?" ME Association, http://www.meassociation.org.uk/about/what-is-mecfs/.

2. Eugene Peterson, *The Jesus Way,* Kindle edition, Loc. 538.

Chapter 8: Extravagant Wastefulness

1. Tim Kreider, "The 'Busy' Trap," *New York Times,* June 30, 2012, http://opinionator.blogs.nytimes.com/2012/06/30/the-busy-trap/?_r=0.

2. Mary Helen Immordino-Yang, et al., "Rest Is Not Idleness," *Perspectives on Psychological Science,* 7:4 (July 2012), http://pps.sagepub.com/content/7/4/352.

3. Emily Young, "What Can Formula One Teach Business Leaders?" *BBC News,* January 16, 2016, http://www.bbc.co.uk/news/business-35363109.

4. About Hinsta Performance, http://www.hintsa.com/about-us/#about-hintsa-performance.

5. Young, "What Can Formula One Teach Business Leaders?"

6. Mark Twain, *Mark Twain's Speeches,* 1923 ed., Introduction.

7. NPR Interview with Terry Gross, "From Walter White to LBJ, Bryan Cranston Is a Master of Transformation," March 27, 2014, http://www.npr.org/2014/03/27/295246908/from-walter-white-to-lbj-bryan-cranston-is-a-master-of-transformation.

8. Daniel Gross, "This Is Your Brain on Silence," *Nautilus,* August 21, 2014, http://nautil.us/issue/16/nothingness/this-is-your-brain-on-silence.

9. Inspired by Henri Nouwen, chap. 2, "Reaching Out" in *A Receptive Solitude* (New York: Doubleday, 1975), 37–38.

10. Brennan Manning, *Ruthless Trust* (New York: Harper Collins, 2000), 115.

11. Laura J. Boggess, *Playdates with God* (Abiline, TX: Leafwood Publishers, 2014), 120.

12. Henri Nouwen, *Reaching Out* (New York: Doubleday, 1975), 34.

13. Brené Brown, *Daring Greatly* (New York: Gotham Books, 2012).

14. Brené Brown, *The Gifts of Imperfection* (Center City, MN: Hazelden, 2010).

15. Ibid.

Chapter 9: Uncertainty: Rest and Love Are Connected

1. Lauren Winner, *Wearing God* (New York: Harper Collins, 2015), 81.

2. Brené Brown, *The Gifts of Imperfection* (Center City, MN: Hazelden, 2010), Kindle edition, Loc. 89.

3. Margaret Feinberg, *Sacred Echo,* Kindle edition, Loc. 385.

4. Ibid., Loc. 409.

Chapter 10: Preparation Is Everything

1. Ann Voskamp, *One Thousand Gifts* (Grand Rapids, MI: Zondervan, 2010), 68.
2. This concept was inspired by Patty Stallings' great questions in a blog post at VelvetAshes.com, "Pleasant Boundary Lines," November 5, 2015, http ://velvetashes.com/pleasant-boundary-lines/.
3. Buchanan, *The Rest of God*, 76–84.
4. Anna Sewell, "The Sunday Cab" and "The Golden Rule," in *Black Beauty*, Kindle, ch. 36, 37.
5. Henri Nouwen, *Out of Solitude*, Kindle edition, Loc. 12.
6. Buchanan, *The Rest of God*.
7. Sewell, *Black Beauty*, Kindle Loc., 156.
8. Ibid., Loc. 158.
9. Voskamp, *One Thousand Gifts*, 124.

Chapter 11: L'Chaim! To Life!

1. Ariela Pelaia, "What Is Challah?" About Religion, January 29, 2016, http:// judaism.about.com/od/jewishculture/a/whatischallah.htm.
2. Brett McCracken, *Gray Matters* (Grand Rapids, MI: Baker Books, 2013), 43.
3. Micha Boyett, "On Friendship and God's Bounty," Grace Table, January 23, 2015, http://gracetable.org/friendship-gods-bounty/.

Chapter 12: Wings of Rescue

1. Mark 3:1–6; Luke 13:10–17; Matthew 12:10.
2. "Free Climbers Reach El Capitan Peak and Make History," *BBC News*, January 15, 2015, http://www.bbc.co.uk/news/world-us-canada-30824372.
3. Henri Nouwen, *Out of Solitude*, Kindle edition, Loc. 328.
4. Preston Yancey, *Tables in the Wilderness* (Grand Rapids, MI: Zondervan, 2014).
5. Andrew Murray, *Waiting on God* (New York: Fleming H. Revell, 1896), 103–104.
6. Oliver Moody, "Free Yourself From Digital Slavery—for a Day at Least," *The Times*, October 17, 2014, http://www.thetimes.co.uk/tto/faith/article4240471.ece.
7. Buechner, *Listening to Your Life*, 332.

Shelly Miller is a veteran ministry leader and sought-after mentor on Sabbath-keeping. She leads the Sabbath Society, an online community of people who want to make rest a priority. Her writing has been featured in multiple books and national publications. Described as a poet with an acute taste for authentic honesty, she is a storyteller who makes people think differently about life. An expat living in London, England, she and her husband, H, are the proud parents of two children.

Find more of Shelly's writing and join the Sabbath Society community at ShellyMillerWriter.com; Instagram and Twitter: @shellymillerwriter; Facebook: Shelly Miller, Writer. #Sabbath-Society and #RhythmsOfRest in community.